SINGER

SEWING REFERENCE LIBRARY®

Sewing Update No. 2

Cy DeCosse Incorporated
Minnetonka, Minnesota

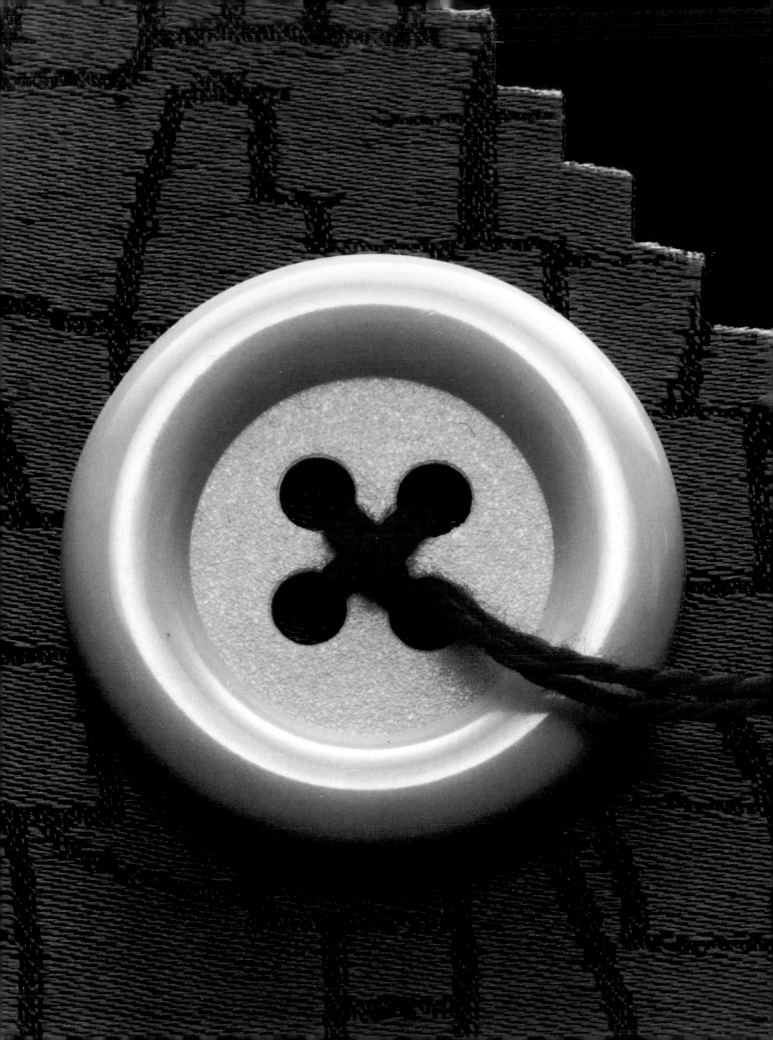

SINGER

SEWING REFERENCE LIBRARY®

Sewing Update

No.2

SINGER

SEWING REFERENCE LIBRARY®

Sewing Update
No. 2

Contents

Copyright © 1989
Cy DeCosse Incorporated
5900 Green Oak Drive
Minnetonka, Minnesota 55343
All rights reserved
Printed in U.S.A.

Also available from the publisher: *Sewing Essentials, Sewing for the Home, Clothing Care & Repair, Sewing for Style, Sewing Specialty Fabrics, Sewing Activewear, The Perfect Fit, Timesaving Sewing, More Sewing for the Home, Sewing Update No. 1, Tailoring, Sewing for Children, Sewing with an Overlock*

Distributed by: Contemporary Books, Inc.
  Chicago, Illinois

ISSN 1040-2985
ISBN 0-86573-245-0
ISBN 0-86573-246-9 (pbk.)
SEWING UPDATE NO. 2
Created by: The Editors of Cy DeCosse Incorporated, in cooperation with the Singer Education Department. Singer is a trademark of The Singer Company and is used under license.

Credits

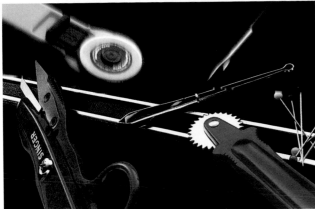

CY DE COSSE INCORPORATED
Chairman: Cy DeCosse
President: James B. Maus
Executive Vice President: William B. Jones

Project Director: Rita C. Opseth
Project Manager: Melissa Erickson
Editorial Director: Nancy Restuccia
Senior Art Director: Lisa Rosenthal
Editors: Janice Cauley, Phyllis Galbraith, Bernice Maehren
Sample Supervisors: Wendy Fedie, Joanne Wawra
Technical Photo Director: Bridget Haugh
Sewing Staff: Phyllis Galbraith, Mary Gannon, Bridget Haugh, Helen Adelsman, Mary Ann Bucklin, Joan Coop, Sheila Duffy, Connie Garritsen, Julie Muschamp, Carol Neumann, Carol Olson, Lori Ritter, Valerie Ruthardt, Nancy Sundeen, Margaret Ulwelling, Barbara Vik, John Wilcox
Fabric Editor: Marie Castle
Photo Studio Manager: Cathleen Shannon
Photographers: Rex Irmen, Tony Kubat, John Lauenstein, Bill Lindner, Mark Macemon, Mette Nielsen, Allen Beaulieu, Bobbette Destiche, Nick Felice, Stefano Grisci, Dan Halsey, Chuck Nields, Steve Olson, Richard Wiseman
Production Manager: Jim Bindas
Assistant Production Managers: Julie Churchill, Jacquie Marx
Production Staff: Russell Beaver, Holly Clements, Sheila DiPaola, Joe Fahey, Kevin D. Frakes, Yelena Konrardy, Scott Lamoureux, Robert Lynch, Linda Schloegel, Greg Wallace, Nik Wogstad
Consultants: Roberta Carr, David Page Coffin, Kathleen Ellingson, Mary Goettelmann, Zoe Graul, Linda Turner Griepentrog, Marit Lee Kucera, Lotus Stack
Contributers: American Efrid; AZ Industries; Blue Feather Products; Clotilde; Clover Needlecraft, Inc.; Creative Fibers; The Crowning Touch, Inc.; Crystal Tissue Company; Distlefink Designs, Inc.; Dritz Corporation; G-Street Fabrics; Gingher, Inc.; HAPCO Products; Homebound Company; June Tailor, Inc.; Kreinik Manufacturing Company; Métier de Gèneve, Elna, Inc.; Minnetonka Mills; Nancy's Notions, Ltd.; Olfa; Paco Despacio; Scandia Down; Sew-Art International; The Singer Company; Special Effects; Speed Stitch; Stacy Industries, Inc.; Tacony Corporation; Treadleart; United Notions; Velcro USA, Inc.; W. H. Collins, Inc.; YLI Corporation
Contributing Photographers: Susan Gilmore; Minneapolis Institute of Arts; Sharon Risedorph; Waverly, Division of F. Shumacher & Co.
Color Separations: Spectrum, Inc.
Printing: W. A. Krueger (0689)

Sewing for Today

Sewing Update No. 2 is dedicated to bringing you all the latest information on fabrics, equipment, trends, and techniques for wearable fashions, home fashions, and fiber arts.

Use this book for ideas and inspiration. Step-by-step instructions are given for most projects. Use them to learn a new skill; then put that skill to use in your next sewing project. Although the articles are grouped by topics, they do not need to be read in any particular order. Skim the pages at your leisure, stopping to examine a new home decorating topic, a fashion sewing skill, or a surface design technique in greater depth, as the fancy strikes you.

New Horizons

The first section contains articles of general interest. Use the information on current trends in fashion and fabrics to update your wardrobe and accessories. There is also an article on how to teach your own child to sew.

Tools of the Trade

As a sewer, you want current information on the latest in sewing machines, sergers, knitting machines, accessories, and notions. This section brings you up to date.

Keeping pace with new techniques and technologies can help you make the most of your sewing time. New computerized sewing machines, electronic knitting machines, and sergers increase the speed and efficiency with which we can work. Some new sewing notions, too, make many tedious aspects of sewing faster and easier; others open new creative possibilities. Sewing machine accessories — many of which you already own — add a whole new dimension to sewing, once you unlock the secrets of their potential.

Surface Design

The hottest topic in sewing today is surface design. Surface design includes all the techniques that add color and texture to a plain expanse of fabric.

The current interest in surface design is at once a look back and a look forward. It is a revival of the historical impulse to lavish attention on fabric, harking back to the days when textiles were among the most expensive of all possessions, and their embellishment a way of flaunting wealth. At the same time, it is a totally contemporary expression of individuality, a way of creating something unique in a world overflowing with mass-produced multiples.

This section contains several articles to whet your appetite for surface design. A number of techniques and ideas are presented, including ruching, marbling, dyeing, and appliquéing. The concluding article tells you how to handle and care for your works of fiber art, to preserve them for future generations. References are included in each article to direct you to further sources of information.

Wearable Fashions

Wearables are the backbone of most home sewer's interest in sewing. Wearables are what most sewers sew. In this section, you will learn new sewing techniques, including quick-and-easy methods for sewing the new spandex stretch-knit fabrics, and for creating sweaters using a construction method called "knit, cut, and sew."

Get inspired! Learn how to copy a ready-to-wear detail. Think about making a garment in this season's show-stopper fabric: lace. If you are among the one-third of the women in this country who wear large sizes, rejoice! The fashion industry is finally catching on, and the selection of patterns and styles has never been better. Or, challenge yourself to improve sewing skills. A lesson in couture techniques for sewing sleeves will bring out your best.

Home Fashions

Sewing for the home can be quick, simple, and rewarding. This section will tell you what the trends are, and how to plan a decorating scheme to update your existing decor. Redo your bedroom with the latest bed skirt and pillow sham design. You will also find step-by-step instructions for dressing up folding chairs with simple slipcovers.

Our Writers

Our writers are experts. Most earn their living doing what they have written about; others, from their ability to seek out the very best sources and convey that information clearly.

We are dedicated to bringing the home sewer up-to-date information that will ensure sewing successes, offer inspiration, and give sewing the savvy, chic image it deserves.

New Horizons

Fabric Outlook

by Molly O'Sullivan

Sewing a garment is a process involving many steps, beginning with an idea and then transforming the idea into reality. In this process, the selection of materials can be the most exciting step.

Sewers love to shop for fabric. The fabrics themselves inspire ideas — by their color, texture, design, drape, even by their location in the fabric store. A fabric shopper uses hands, eyes, emotions, and experience to select just the right fabric for a project.

Fabric shopping can be a very creative process. A garment takes shape in the sewer's mind as she touches different fabrics, the fibers gliding or resisting, crumpling or falling softly, each according to its own unique character. This mental process is so real that often a sewer will buy more fabric than she has time to use, because the garments "exist" so plainly in her mind. Some fabrics become old friends before they are cut and prepared for construction! In the ideal situation, however, concept, fabric, pattern, shears, and sewing machine all come together in short order to create a finished garment.

Daywear Choices

Today's home sewer demands quality and durability from her fabrics, as well as aesthetic appeal; she wants fabrics that are worthy of the time and effort spent on construction. These "investment fabrics" provide the basis for an enduring and versatile daytime wardrobe. Fortunately, there is a wide selection of high-quality fabrics from which to choose.

New this year for home sewing are silk gabardines, available in a broad range of colors. They work well for almost any type of garment, particularly for jackets, skirts, and slacks. Mini-wardrobes of mix-and-match coordinates could be created by combining smooth-textured silk gabardines with rough-surfaced silk tweeds that have the look of handwovens.

Because today's woman wants to move freely in her clothing, she welcomes the wide selection of contemporary knit fabrics available. These are not the polyester double knits of old! Instead, cotton, wool, and luxury cashmere fibers in both single and double knits mix easily into a professional wardrobe that remains fresh and wrinkle-free throughout the long working day.

Since the development of acrylics and polyesters, very few new fibers have come to market for home sewers; rather, existing fibers have been refined. Some of the most innovative refinements are in the synthetic suedes category.

The original Ultrasuede® by Skinner has been on the market since 1970, and has maintained a strong position in fabric stores for most of that time. This polyester and polyurethane fabric has been modified in recent years, and now luxury Facile® and Caress™ are available to the home sewer. Caress is the lightest of the Ultrasuede family, with the drape and hand of a natural skin. Caress weighs only four ounces (114 g) per square yard (.95 m), is available in 17 colors, and lends itself to draped, gathered, and softly pleated garments. The appeal of Ultrasuede products is twofold: the beauty of its color and texture, and its total practicality. It is remarkable that a suede of such realistic appearance can be machine washed and dried — a real asset to the fashion-conscious home sewer.

Rayon is experiencing a resurgence in popularity. Because it is made from cellulose, rayon has many qualities of a natural fiber fabric even though it is manufactured. It breathes, wrinkles, shrinks, and drapes like linens and cottons, but it has its very own look, both distinguishable and desirable.

Rayon is available in a wide range of textures. The printed crepes are most reminiscent of those available in its heyday, bringing back the look of the 1940s. Rayon challis is a reasonably priced and great-looking alternative to its wool counterpart; its appeal is its fine hand and exquisite colorations. As a substitute for pure linen, handsome structured rayon tweed suitings are perfect for warmer seasons.

Polyester has ridden a roller coaster of popularity since its development. First seen as the ultimate easy-care fiber, it was produced in great volume for sportswear knits and texturized wovens. It nearly took over fabric stores in the 1970s. Then, sewers began to prefer natural fiber fabrics, and for some time polyester was considered unworthy of the serious sewer's attention.

Now, polyester has regained acceptance, and for good reasons. It is indeed an easy-care fabric, excellent for travel as well as for working wardrobes. The silky polyesters, such as jacquards, crepe de chine prints, and tissue failles, are reasonable and attractive silk substitutes. In addition, polyester is the ultimate "blender," combining its best qualities with natural fibers for maximum benefit. Poly and wool; poly and cotton; poly and linen; poly, cotton, and spandex; poly and rayon — in each of these combinations, polyester adds its distinctive benefits of easy care, resilience, and practicality.

For designer use in particular, wool fabrics are in the limelight. Always a part of cool-weather wardrobes, wools now are used in everything from resort wear to evening wear. Pure wool is often combined with cashmere, polyester, angora, and, most recently, spandex for a wide range of effects and prices.

The hard-finish worsted woolens, such as gabardine, tropical wool, and menswear, are best suited to all-season use. These investment fabrics are ideal for the working woman, who needs clothes that can endure changes in fashion as well as the wear and tear of daily use.

A less traditional, more colorful, potential for an office wardrobe can be found in the vast variety of silk tweed suitings available. Their highly sophisticated colorations and handwoven appearance lend a one-of-a-kind look to the serious office uniform.

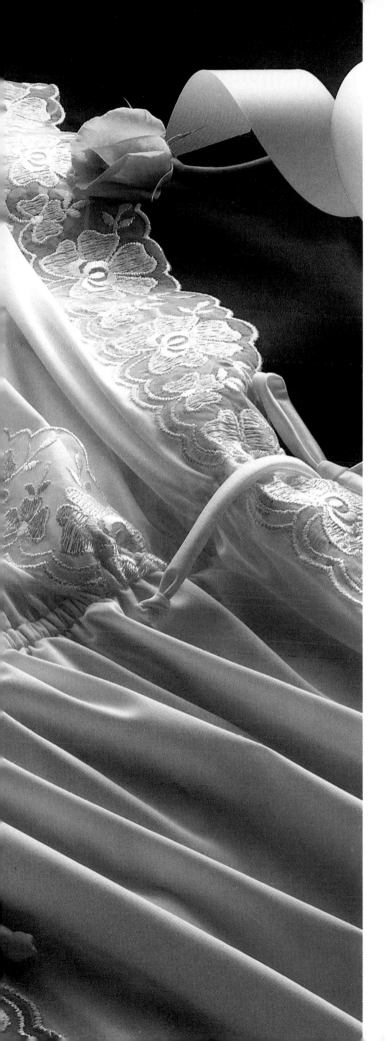

Evening Wear Choices

For evening wear, the most significant fashion statement is made by lace. As a whole garment, embellishment, or trim, lace is the most cherished and elegant fabric for special-occasion dressing. Laces are generally 36" (91.5 cm) wide, and most come with both edges scalloped, so that a bodice with its own finish can easily be designed. Chantilly laces often are reembroidered with ribbon, organza, or soutache braid to add dimension and texture to an already-interesting fabric surface. For even greater opulence, laces are available with applied beads and sequins, either to match or to contrast with the color of the lace.

Textured silks, such as matelassé and cloque, stage a comeback on today's fabric scene. These dimensional fabrics provide tone-on-tone surface appeal for special-occasion styles ranging from simple to elegant.

Specialty Choices

A whole world of materials lays in wait for the industrious and creative home sewer who makes lingerie and activewear. There now are patterns, notions, and fabrics for sewing the entire range of intimate apparel, from bras to negligees. Satin-faced flannel — a woven polyester, cotton, and nylon blend — is ideal for robes and nightgowns due to its unique brushed flannel and satin construction. Nylon tricot, which is available in 15-denier and 40-denier weights, is suitable for camisoles, slips, and panties.

Swimsuits are simple and economical to construct, and, fortunately, swimwear fabrics are abundant and exotic. Floral prints, textured solids, and metallic embossed animal prints provide a range of possibilities to the interested sewer.

Creative sewing options exist for activewear as well, and the new cotton and Lycra® knits add the most recent dimension to this category. Perfect for leotards, unitards, and even sportswear dressing, this fabric is comfortable — it moves with the body and breathes during workouts. For the serious biker or exercise fan who sews, heavy-duty satin Lycra is a good choice for cycling pants, tights, and swimsuits.

The fabric news is clear: an abundance of fabric choices assures home sewers that they can find suitable materials for whatever projects they undertake in the months ahead.

Molly O'Sullivan has been general manager of G Street Fabrics since 1982. She is a member of the Washington, D.C., Fashion Group and is on the Board of the American Home Sewing Association.

Fashion Forecast

by Lisa Lebowitz

Today's fashion message? In a word, femininity. No matter where you live — in the country or the city, in a cold climate or warm — feminine touches grace clothing, from the most citified, serious suit to the easiest, beachbound pants.

This type of femininity should not be confused with the sexy fashion message of seasons past: body-clinging dresses, thigh-baring skirts, and underwear worn as outerwear. Instead, clothes are comfortable and flattering. Soft and pretty replaces tight and restrictive, making the months ahead ones of very wearable — and very sewable — clothes.

Now, there is more reason to sew than ever. Thanks to a new sophistication in the pattern industry, fashion trends are translated into sewable looks the very year they appear on designer runways and in ready-to-wear lines. And patterns now accommodate the home sewer's time limitations — all major pattern companies offer quick-sew options.

Career Clothes

Jackets remain a career-dressing staple. For cold weather, menswear wools are ideal. Tweeds, pinstripes, chalk-stripes, and herringbones give jackets office impact. A jacket can be authoritative, yet still be feminine and flattering, when accessorized with feminine details like lace edging, white collars and cuffs, or a chiffon pocket square.

In color, many of this year's wools are traditionally sober in navys, blacks, and grays. Fabric designers are also using red as a new neutral "power color" for career dressing.

The pants suit will be seen in many offices. In particular, pants with fuller legs look feminine and new, with soft pleats or tucks that keep the tummy area looking flat. Or, a jacket may be paired with wool shorts that are tailored and slim. "The Bermuda

shorts suit is important," says Cindy Rose, Fashion Director for Vogue/Butterick patterns. "A jacket and walking shorts create a sophisticated look this year."

As the weather warms, look for jackets in flowing trapeze styles. These loose, triangular toppers join cropped, waist-length, and hip-grazing styles as this year's favorites, says Rose. In lightweight, year-round wools and crisp cottons, they are new wardrobe basics.

"Soft" is the word for skirts. Now they are made from drapable wool, challis, or gabardine. Fashion experts are calling skirts "rounder," with more of a curve at the hips — another earmark of femininity — and a slightly pegged bottom.

Crisp white cotton blouses will top pants and skirts. According to Sidney Tepper, Vice President and Design Director for The McCall Pattern Company, classic man-tailored blouses include surprising feminine touches, like contrast embroidery or rows of rick-rack on plackets or collars. Three-quarter-length sleeves on dresses and blouses update last year's looks.

Dresses will be important at the office, particularly when the weather turns hot. Look for dresses that are suit-inspired. Not to be confused with two-piece dressing, "suit-dresses," says Lee Hogan Cass, Vice President and Fashion Director for The Broadway, a major retail store in Los Angeles, "have the appearance of a jacket on top, but they're usually made of a soft, feminine fabric, like a beautiful silk." The tops are slightly elongated and fitted, but not tight; skirts are knee-length and straight, or long and full.

The coatdress is another reliable classic, and a cool, authoritative alternative to dressing in suit layers. This year, look for newsworthy covered buttons on linen and gabardine coatdresses.

The shaped sheath and the soft chemise, classic feminine shapes, reappear on the fashion scene with the warm weather. The look is Jackie O. with a twist — bright colors emerge more strongly this year, bringing these styles right up to date. Princess and A-line shifts are other important dress shapes. Topped with a cropped or hip-length jacket, these dresses are well suited for office wear.

Details and accessories become a fashion focus when there is no startling change in overall silhouette from one year to the next. For your career wardrobe this year, according to Cindy Rose, contrast buttons are important, as are fine, natural buttons like tortoise-shell and horn. Also, watch for contour stitching and elastic insets. "Clothes this year are more classic than trendy," says Rose. "They are cleaned up, with an emphasis on fine styling in the true Milanese or French tradition."

Overall, emphasis moves from the shoulder to the neckline. Shoulder pads are smaller, defining the shoulder rather than exaggerating it. Neckline and collar details add feminine interest to career clothing. White cotton blouses with U-shaped, sweetheart, or fichu (scarf) necklines add a soft-dressing note to slim, classic skirts and trousers. Portrait collars, which create a sort of picture frame around the face, enhance dresses and blouses. "These styles flatter the wearer, drawing attention upward," says Sidney Tepper.

Accessories are as feminine as the clothes they accompany. "This year, you might wear a cluster of antique pins on the lapel of a suit jacket," says Tracey Battista, Accessories Editor at *Glamour* magazine. "Accessories are elaborate, with semiprecious stones like garnet, carnelian, lapis, and onyx, and these stones are set in burnished or antiqued gold settings." The way to accessorize portrait collars, for example, is with a pin — burnished, with semiprecious stones — rather than a necklace. The best earrings are long drops, like a beautiful pair with black onyx beads, Battista adds.

Charm bracelets are important, also in burnished gold. Filigree pins, hoop earrings that are braided for a slightly ethnic flavor, and slim, structured bags add feminine polish to updated classic clothing. The newest-looking handbag to go with suits this year is a modified Grace Kelly purse, the kind with handles and — the new detail — a matching shoulder strap. Gone are sloppy slouch bags, replaced by smaller, ladylike purses with a bit more structure.

Suede belts make news for cold-weather clothes, and the belt to buy, if you buy just one, is two inches wide with gold hardware or a simple covered buckle. Footwear is simple in woven slip-ons or matte leathers and suedes.

Hats are more feminine than in the past few years, too. Last season, at the first sign of a chill, you might have placed a felt fedora squarely on your head; this year, you may reach instead for a beret or a modified pillbox. If you prefer to go hatless, think chiffon. A wisp of this fabric tied around your ponytail looks fresh and pretty, and echoes the chiffon pocket square you might wear with your jacket.

Dressy Occasions

When festivities are planned, clothes become decidedly feminine by virtue of both fabric and styling. Opulent tapestry brocades, velvets, elaborate laces, and autumn-leaf-toned paisleys make even the simplest A-line dress or unadorned pants look rich.

Cropped jackets frequently top skirts or trousers that have a slightly higher waistband, or an all-out Empire line. Because the Empire waist is hard for many women to wear, "we've created patterns for slim skirts and pants with modified Empire waists," explains Sidney Tepper. "They're more comfortable and more flattering to most figures." The net effect is an hourglass shape that is decidedly feminine.

Tuxedo pants in black or gray with a satin stripe down the side are a new force in black-tie dressing. Soft styles in black crepe, silk, or satin are always nighttime favorites when topped by a special blouse in white satin or charmeuse.

Holiday and special-occasion dressing is in turn Romantic, Baroque, or Edwardian, inspired in part by art exhibitions recently touring Europe, like London's "Age of Chivalry," and the Degas, Van Gogh, and Winterhalter shows in Paris. Even shoes relect this trend. Graceful Louis heels look feminine and romantic in suede.

In accessories, "look for crosses and crests, and elaborate Baroque or heraldic pieces," says Battista. Suede accessories are dark and rich in eggplant, purple, and hunter green. In keeping with the romantic spirit, gloves and hats are trimmed in fur for cold-weather occasions. Burnished buttons, tassels, lace, jet beads, and embroidery are everywhere. Satin rosettes, bows, and scrollwork further adorn holiday shoes.

Casual Dressing

While casual "Country Romance" looks will not debut in many offices, they are perfect for warm, balmy nights and sunny weekends.

Weekend dresses are new-looking, but with a distinctly 1950s' flavor. Thanks to Brigitte Bardot, off-the-shoulder shapes have feminine allure.

Chemises and sundresses, as well as tiered ethnic-looking skirts that combine floral and patterned prints, make a strong showing with the warmer weather. Feminine florals in pastels and brights blossom into short, flirty skirts and long, flowing styles.

The blouses that top these looks are innocent and romantic, with covered buttons and fichu or portrait necklines. The same blouses can top easy, full-legged trousers that have a nautical flare at the bottom for warm weather. Add a face-framing, wide-brimmed hat, and the look is pretty as a picture.

In this category of warm-weather clothes, brights look particularly fresh, focusing on fuchsias, pinks, oranges, and brilliant blues. Pastels are another option for colors that span the spectrum of soft and pretty.

According to Cindy Rose, watch for brightly colored, satin-ribbon bow appliqués everywhere — from small ones in many colors scattered across the front of a sweater, to a row of monochromatic bows parading around the bottom of a gown, to a single large bow finishing the satin-ribbon neckline of an off-the-shoulder dress. Fabric roses, ruffled laces, and embroidered eyelet trims complement country looks, adding to the feminine feel.

Expect accessories for casual dressing to pick up the floral theme, with rosettes on earrings, hair accessories, and straw boaters. Shoes, too, carry through the Country Romance look. Brightly colored leather pumps and flats showcase gardens of rosettes, collections of bows, contrast piping, or other trims. Ballerina flats are the perfect footnote to many of this year's feminine dresses. Also from the 1950s, look for vintage sunglasses, trims, and feminine straw or wicker purses with handles.

Lisa Lebowitz is a New York City-based freelance writer and syndicated columnist who frequently writes on fashion and beauty. She formerly wrote the pattern page for Glamour *magazine.*

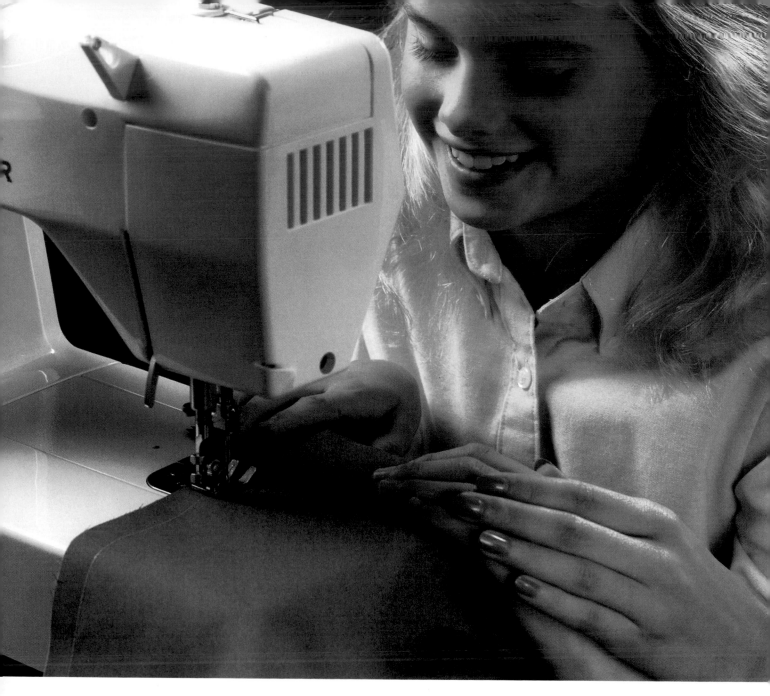

Teaching Your Child to Sew

by Cindra Halm

For many sewing enthusiasts, earliest memories include the whir of a machine, the heat of an iron, and the colors of fabric scraps on a table. Perhaps you remember more personal sensations: Mom pulling a half-made dress over your head, or Aunt Mary showing off the newest section of her quilt. If yours was a sewing family, you grew up surrounded by the tools of the trade, everything from bobbins to buttons. Then, at some point, you began to help pin patterns. You ironed seams flat. You crumpled fabric between your fingers.

A Valuable Heritage

These memories may be nostalgic, but they represent your heritage. Or, if you are a first-generation sewer, you could be creating such a heritage for your children. Like mother, like daughter or son; your children want to sew, and you want to teach them to enjoy the craft as much as you do. You want to share your skills, to guide your child's natural curiosity and blossoming creativity. This is the sewing legacy.

Sewing instruction has returned to the home. With the virtual disappearance of home economics classes in schools and a return to traditional forms in all the arts, more people are teaching sewing in their homes. Sewing affords a wonderful opportunity for children to enjoy family time together, as well as to develop pride in themselves. Children can gain valuable feelings of belonging, purpose, and accomplishment as projects for the family and gifts for friends and relatives are made, used, and admired.

Tips for Teaching Children

Your children sense it, and you know it: Sewing is fun! But, how do you go about teaching them the actual skills involved? As a general rule, be available but not overbearing in your instruction, and watch their cues. They have their own pace, taste, and talents.

The following specific advice for teaching children to sew comes from teachers, designers, and others who are expert at working with children.

• Share your enthusiasm. You love to sew; this is one of your greatest assets in leading your child to appreciate both the process and the products of your craft. Enthusiasm is contagious! Use it to motivate and sustain your child's interest at all levels of instruction. This does not mean you have to be excessively bubbly or full of tricks. The key to teaching is loving the work and letting your children know it.

• Help your child to become comfortable with the sewing machine. Your child wants to sew. But what first? Start by encouraging familiarity with and respect for the machine. Let the child practice, to build confidence. Tracing simple designs on paper or pre-printed fabric, using an unthreaded needle, is a valuable first exercise for learning control. Then let the child sew with thread on many types of fabric, in order to feel the different weights and tensions. Use contrasting thread to help illustrate stitch type and length, and how a stitch is formed.

• Ease problems with patience. A consistent stumbling block for children ages six to ten, whose motor skills are still developing, is threading the machine. In this case you can thread the machine yourself, with confidence, and allow the child to observe. Eventually, the child will want to try threading it, and will learn, despite a few inevitable mistakes.

• Use the child's language. Patterns children can read and understand are important to the success of a project. For children to follow a pattern, the instructions should be large, clear, and marked with obvious signals for folding, cutting, and matching. You may want to check your local fabric store or the advertisements in your favorite sewing publications for patterns written especially for children.

• Explain the process of cutting and sewing the garment in simple terms — then let your child do it. Leave the room if you have to! Resist the temptation to jump in and sew the project yourself when questions arise. Demonstrate on scrap fabric rather than on the child's project if you need to show how to do something.

• Start small, and keep it simple. The sooner children are able to reap the benefits of their work, the more likely they are to continue and to expand their interest. The best beginning projects are those that use a straight stitch, a minimum of sewing machine attachments, and easy-to-handle, nonslipping fabrics. A pillow, baggy shorts, a tote bag, or a straight skirt make good small, practical projects for a novice.

• Involve children right from the start; take them shopping with you to help select pattern and fabric. Remember, children have their own preferences for style, which must be considered. Too much rigidity on your part is likely to stifle curiosity and enthusiasm. You want your child to want to learn. One happily finished project will nurture the desire for another.

• Maintain a sense of humor and perspective. Of course, children learn from their mistakes, and when the inevitable happens, shared stories about your own goofs can help.

• Keep an eye out for potential problems, such as threading or tension. Help prevent them, to spare your child the frustration of a jammed machine. A tactful reminder can prevent sewn-together pockets. A good rule is to do as little ripping as possible. In the early stages of learning, discouragement comes easily. Be attentive. The aim at this level is not perfection, but completion. It is the magic that happens when fabric becomes garment, when something wished becomes something realized.

A child who grows up around sewing is surrounded by color and texture, by knowledge and creativity, by patience and love. It is a rich legacy. Memories are housed not only in photos or stories, but passed through hands, like quilts, from one generation to the next.

Cindra Halm, poet and freelance writer from Minneapolis, is now enrolled in the Graduate Creative Writing Program at Hollins College. She has worked with and cared for children of all ages.

Tools of the Trade

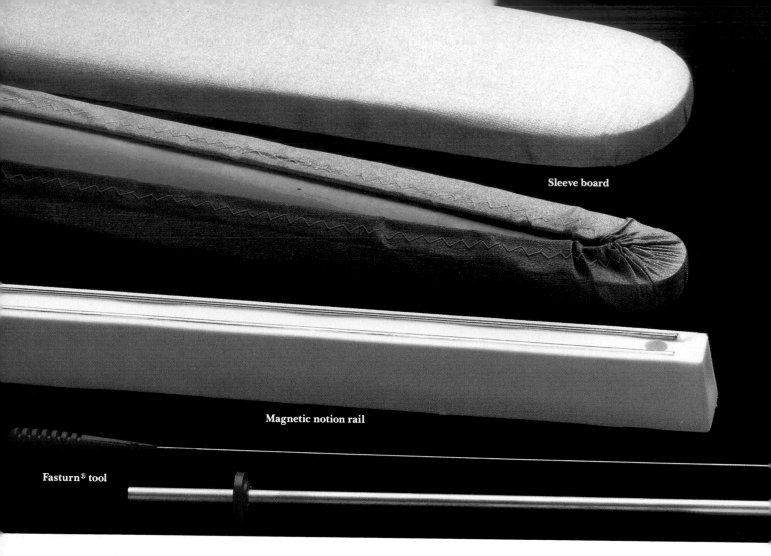

Sleeve board

Magnetic notion rail

Fasturn® tool

New Notions

by Janet Klaer

Lucky for us sewers, many exciting new notions are introduced each year. Some save us time, others give us better-looking results, and some just make sewing more fun by eliminating tedious steps. Here is a collection of twelve notions that I found to be the best of this year's crop. Look for them at your favorite fabric store or from your sewing machine dealer. Many are also available through notions mail-order companies.

Chaco-liner by Clover Needlecraft, Inc., is a new chalk marking wheel. It is shaped like a pencil, so it is comfortable to use and easy to maneuver. A serrated wheel in the narrow tip rotates to produce a fine powdered chalk line.

The Chaco-liner is available in white, pink, yellow, and blue. The leakproof case has a screw-on cap that

prevents powder leakage, keeps out moisture, and makes it easy to refill. The chalk brushes away and will not stain your fabric. It is also washable.

Use the Chaco-liner to mark cutting lines, stitching lines, and construction details, such as center front, center back, grainlines, and foldlines. With the fine tip of the Chaco-liner you can get right next to a ruler or template, or in between the lines of a quilting stencil. When marking an exact point, make an "X" with the Chaco-liner.

One-step Needle Threader by Clotilde looks like a big needle itself. It is a flexible wire with a loop at one end and a point at the other, so fine it will go through the eye of almost all machine and hand sewing needles. Use it also for threading the guides and loopers on a serger, and the bobbin tension bypass hole on some conventional sewing machines.

This threader is easy to use. First, insert the thread into the wire loop. Then, insert the wire point into the eye or hole and pull it through. Clotilde's threader works with any thread, but it is especially useful for

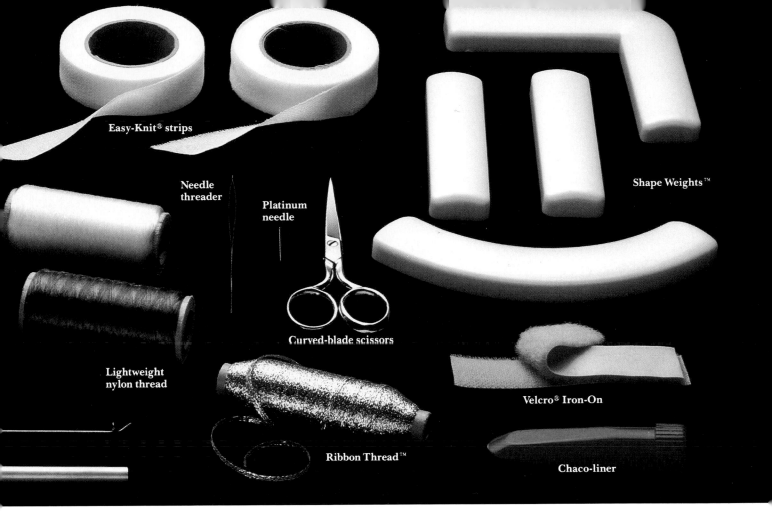

Easy-Knit® strips

Needle threader

Platinum needle

Shape Weights™

Curved-blade scissors

Lightweight nylon thread

Velcro® Iron-On

Ribbon Thread™

Chaco-liner

difficult threads, such as woolly nylon, which is fluffy; invisible thread, which can be hard to see; and thick decorative threads, such as ribbon thread and pearl cotton.

Perhaps the only problem you could ever have with this threader is losing it — and it even comes with a magnetic strip to lessen that possibility!

Magnetic notions continue to increase in popularity. Notion rails keep frequently used sewing tools organized and within easy reach. Magnetic wrist and tabletop pin holders have become indispensable for many sewers. Magnetic seam guides are an aid to straight seams and topstitching.

As the use of magnetic tools increases, so does the concern about whether these items affect our watches and computerized sewing machines. As a general rule, magnets the size and strength of those used in sewing notions will not affect computerized sewing machines. They are small and not very strong, compared to most magnets. Their magnetic field is usually short and concentrated.

According to most sewing machine manufacturers, magnetic notions will not affect their computerized machines, because the area where the computer chip is located is well insulated and shielded. They have designed their machines to avoid this problem. In some computerized sewing machines, magnets are even part of the inner workings of the machine.

However, to all general rules there are exceptions. A few sewing machine manufacturers expressed some concern regarding magnetic notions. Therefore, treat magnetic notions with care. It is best not to stick magnetic items directly on computerized machines. If your computerized sewing machine does a stitch you did not ask for, or if you should lose a pattern, check to see if there is a magnet nearby.

It is advisable to remove your watch when using a magnetic wrist pin holder (or wear it on the opposite wrist). A magnet could cause a battery-operated watch to lose time or stop altogether. With an old-fashioned wind-up watch, there are steel parts inside that could become magnetized, causing damage.

Fasturn® by Crowning Touch, Inc., is a new sewing tool for turning fabric loops and tubes. The Fasturn is a hollow brass cylinder with a specially designed thin wire hook. The cylinders are available in six sizes, ranging from ⅛" to ¾" (3 mm to 2 cm) in diameter.

Finally, somebody has figured out how to make the tedious and often frustrating task of turning loops easy! In seconds, you can turn yards of tiny tubes to make spaghetti straps, button loops, or Chinese ball buttons. Or, stuff larger fabric tubes with cording to make belts, baskets, wreaths, or curtain tie-backs.

In addition to cording, you can stuff fabric tubes with belting, elastic, or yarn while you turn them. Instructions for making the belt, pictured above, are available from Crowning Touch, Inc.

Or, turn fleece-stuffed flat tubes. Weave the tubes together to create an interesting fabric. Use it to make anything from a placemat to a vest, or for decorative details like pockets and yokes on clothing. For a fast and easy baby quilt, sew the tubes together side by side using a decorative machine stitch, and edge the whole thing with lace. The possibilities are virtually endless.

Sleeve Board by June Tailor is now available in a "free-arm" style. A U-shaped metal support holds the two boards together at one end. This makes it possible to press open an entire sleeve seam at one time. Although this sleeve board is indispensable for pressing sleeves, do not limit its use. Use it also as a mini-ironing board to press any area of a garment that does not fit smoothly over a regular ironing board.

Since one side of the sleeve board is narrower than the other, it is ideal for pressing small openings, construction details, and children's clothing. Use the wider side for touch-up pressing. The curved ends of the board are perfect for pressing sleeve caps. For additional padding when steaming sleeve caps, slip the pocket of a press mitt over the end of the sleeve board.

Easy-Knit® by Stacy Industries, one of the most popular fusible interfacings, is now available in ¾" (2 cm) strips on 10-yard (9.15-m) rolls. There are two versions: Straight Cut and Bias Cut.

Easy-Knit Straight Cut is stable in the lengthwise direction with just a slight bit of "give." Use it on knit and woven fabrics to stabilize shoulder seams, shaped seams, pocket edges, and zipper areas to prevent them from stretching out of shape. Straight Cut can also be used as a backing under decorative stitching on stretchy or lightweight fabrics.

Easy-Knit Bias Cut adds support, yet it gives and stretches. Use Bias Cut on knit or woven fabrics to add body in the hem area, for example. On a narrow turned-and-stitched hem, Bias Cut also improves the quality of topstitching and helps to eliminate ripples in the hem on full or flared skirts.

How to Use the Fasturn Tool

1) Cut bias strip. Stitch, right sides together, to make tube; continue stitching across one end of tube. Slip fabric tube over the appropriate-size cylinder.

2) Insert wire hook through cylinder and into fabric. Twist hook to the right to hold fabric securely.

3) Pull fabric approximately ½" (1.3 cm) into tube. If cording is desired, insert end of appropriate-size cording.

 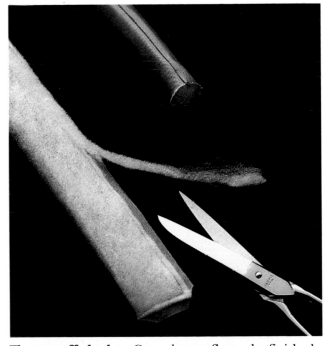

4) Pull hook through brass cylinder. Cording will fill tube as fabric is turned right side out. Twist hook to the left to remove from fabric.

Fleece-stuffed tubes. Cut polyester fleece the finished width of the fabric tube plus a seam allowance. Stitch fleece into seam while stitching tube. Trim fleece seam allowance close to stitches. Turn fabric with fleece, using Fasturn tool.

Ribbon Thread™ by Métier de Gèneve is a narrow rayon ribbon originally used for knitting. Because it is soft and supple, it adapts well for use on the sewing machine.

Ribbon thread is available in solid colors and metallics. Use it to create lustrous decorative edgings and trims for accessories, clothing, and home decorating projects.

On a conventional sewing machine, use ribbon thread in the bobbin, with a matching all-purpose thread or nylon thread in the needle. The best effects are achieved with a long straight stitch or with an outline stitch such as the feather stitch. Ribbon thread does not work well with satin or dense stitches.

On a serger, ribbon thread is most often used in the upper looper of a 3-thread decorative overedge stitch. Use matching serger thread or nylon thread in the needle and lower looper.

Lightweight nylon monofilament thread is a soft and very fine thread, usually .004 mm, or size 80. It is available on 1000-yard (920-m) tubes as well as on 1500-yard (1380-m) and 5400-yard (4968-m) cones. Do not confuse this new thread with "invisible" nylon thread, which is much heavier.

Lightweight nylon thread blends with the fabric so well that it seems to disappear. It is available in clear and smoke. Use clear to sew on whites, pastels, and light to medium colors. Use smoke for grays, blues, and dark colors.

Because lightweight nylon thread is very fine, it is not strong enough for seams and should not be used in areas of stress. It is best for use when all-purpose thread would detract from your decorative stitching or when it is hard to match the color of thread to your fabric.

This lightweight nylon monofilament thread works well on both conventional sewing machines and sergers with little, if any, tension adjustment. Use a size 11/75 or 12/80 needle. If your stitching puckers, loosen the tension.

On a conventional sewing machine, use lightweight nylon thread in the needle and bobbin for quilting, appliqué, and attaching trims or decorative patches.

On a serger, use lightweight nylon thread in the needle, upper looper, and lower looper for sewing rolled hems and blind hems, and for applying pearls or sequins. For decorative edge finishes, use lightweight nylon thread in the needle and lower looper, with your decorative thread in the upper looper.

Platinum-plated needles are ideal for all types of hand sewing, but are especially helpful when sewing for a long period of time. The platinum plating improves the "glide" of the needle, which enables it to go through the fabric with minimum resistance.

In addition, platinum-plated needles will not corrode, rust, or tarnish, even in humid areas. They will not cause an allergic reaction. And, because platinum is highly resistant to body chemicals and oils, the needles will not stain your fingers or leave black marks on your fabric.

The most popular platinum-plated needles are the betweens (sizes 8, 10, and 12) and the tapestry (sizes 18, 20, 22, 24, and 26). Betweens are short needles with small, round eyes, used for fine detailed work such as hand quilting and tailoring. Tapestry needles have blunt points and long, large eyes. Use them for counted cross stitch and needlepoint. When using a thimble, use a leather or nonmetal one to eliminate any possibility of chipping the platinum.

Curved-blade embroidery scissors by Gingher® are designed for cutting threads at the sewing machine, where it is often awkward to cut or difficult to see well. These 4" (10 cm) scissors are particulary helpful when doing decorative stitching, including machine embroidery, quilting, appliqué, cutwork, Battenburg lace, and charted needlework.

When you are cutting with the point of the scissors, a curved blade lets you see your work better. In addition, a curved blade gets your fingertips up off the fabric, so they do not interfere with cutting.

When cutting with the middle of the curve of the blade, you can get the scissors close to the fabric, yet keep the points of the blade slightly off the surface. This helps to ensure that the tips will not accidentally cut into your work.

Sew-Rite® Shape Weights™ are the newest addition to the line of products intended for use in place of pins to hold pattern pieces for cutting. Shape Weights differ from other products in that they are designed to fit common pattern shapes — curves for armholes and necklines, right angles for corners, and bars for straight edges.

Shape Weights can be used with any fabric. They are invaluable for use with fabrics that are difficult to pin or that may be marred by pins.

Velcro® Brand Iron-On Hook & Loop Fastener is a great closure for home decorating, apparel, and craft projects where it is difficult to sew by machine, or where you do not want a stitching line to show. Use it for children's clothing and sportswear, draperies and slipcovers, as well as for repairs and mending.

Velcro Brand Iron-On Hook & Loop Fastener is ¾" (2 cm) wide and is available in white, beige, and black. The special adhesive bonds extremely well when applied according to the directions on the package. It is recommended for use on medium-weight to heavyweight fabrics. It is not compatible with lightweight fabrics, nor should it be used on polyester, rayon, or nylon. Always test on scrap fabric to be sure the adhesive does not bleed through and the fabric does not scorch.

Janet Klaer, formerly Director of Education and Consumer Affairs for Coats & Clark Inc., is a well-known authority on sewing notions, and operates a consulting business.

Specialized Needles & Feet

by Ann Price

There are so many accessories available for sewing machines. I did not fully realize how many until I worked as educational manager for a sewing machine company. There are many kinds of needles, feet, attachments, cams, cassettes, and cartridges.

If you are like most home sewers, you already own your fair share of these accessories. You probably bought them when you bought your sewing machine. And you probably have not used most of them since.

With today's fashion emphasis on creative expression and surface design, the time has come to dust off these sewing aids — maybe even to add a few more to your collection. Specialized needles and feet are particularly easy to overlook because they are so small, but their potential to enhance creativity and to save time is great. Once you get used to using your forgotten feet and neglected needles, you will wonder how you ever sewed without them!

Wing Needles

A glance through any collection of fine table and bed linens reveals examples of the delicate craft of hemstitching. On antique linens, hemstitching was done by hand. Selected threads were drawn out of the fabric, and stitches were taken on the remaining threads to create a variety of lacelike effects. New versions are most often done by machine. Threads may still be drawn out of the fabric but, more often, they are simply pushed aside. The technique is surprisingly easy to do on any zigzag sewing machine. All it takes is a single-wing or double-wing needle.

Wing needles — so named because they appear to have "wings" on their sides — push the threads aside, producing the characteristic "holes" of hemstitched fabric. Double-wing needles feature a wing needle and a standard needle on one shank.

Hemstitching is most successful on delicate, crisp, natural fiber fabrics such as handkerchief linen, organdy, and organza. The fabric must be woven loosely enough so that the wing needle can push the yarns aside without damaging them. And it must have enough body so that the hole made by the needle does not close again immediately afterward.

Wing needle and special-purpose foot are used for hemstitched details shown on blouse and handkerchief.

Hemstitching on the bias or crosswise grain produces a more open look than on the lengthwise grain, so cut out pattern pieces accordingly. For example, if you wish to hemstitch down the center of a blouse, cut that piece on the bias or crosswise grain.

A basic zigzag stitch gives interesting effects when sewn with the single-wing needle. Sew directly on the project, or hemstitch strips or blocks to insert or appliqué to the fashion fabric.

To achieve the look of entredeux, use a double-wing needle and a straight stitch. Sew twice, once up and then back, to get the effect. This is a nice technique for sewing hems or attaching lace.

Special-Purpose Presser Foot

Almost every machine comes with a special-purpose presser foot, sometimes called a satin stitch foot, that has been designed specifically for satin stitching (a very close zigzag). This foot has a wide channel on the underside, behind the needle hole. This creates a "tunnel" through which embroidery and satin stitches can pass without piling up or being flattened.

Depending on the machine, special-purpose feet are available in metal or clear plastic. On some metal feet, the front has been cut away. The clear and open-toed versions make it easier to follow any marked line, as when monogramming, quilting, matching automatic embroidery stitches, or appliquéing.

Take a look in chic ready-to-wear boutiques and mail-order catalogs, and you are bound to collect ideas for elegant applications for your special-purpose foot. One of the most common of these is appliqué, because it can be adapted to suit any age and taste.

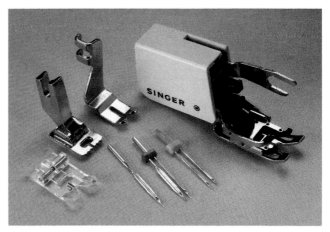

Feet, left to right: special-purpose foot, pin-tuck foot, gathering foot, Even Feed™ foot. Needles, left to right: single-wing needle, double-wing needle, twin needle.

How to Hemstitch Using a Double-Wing Needle & Special-Purpose Presser Foot

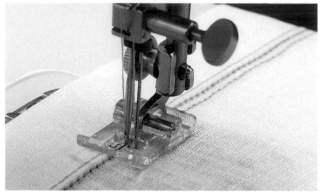

Stitching a hem. 1) Press double-fold hem in sheer fabric. Insert double-wing needle and special-purpose presser foot. From right side, position fabric so standard needle stitches hem edge and wing needle pierces single layer of fabric. Stitch, using straight stitch.

2) Turn fabric at end of stitching. Stitch again; stitch slowly and make sure wing needle enters holes exactly on first line of stitching.

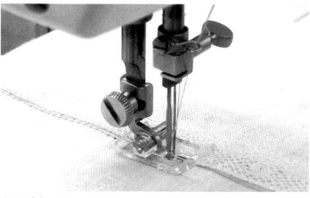

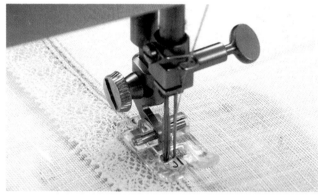

Attaching lace. 1) Insert double-wing needle and special-purpose presser foot. Mark stitching line with chalk. Position straight edge of lace along marked line. Stitch, using straight stitch with standard needle piercing edge of lace and wing needle piercing fabric only.

2) Turn fabric at end of stitching. Stitch again; stitch slowly and make sure wing needle enters holes exactly on first line of stitching.

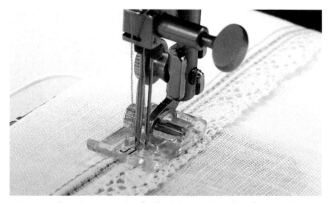

Stitching hem with lace. 1) Press double-fold hem in sheer fabric. Insert double-wing needle and special-purpose presser foot. From right side, position fabric so standard needle stitches hem edge and wing needle pierces single layer of fabric. Stitch, using straight stitch.

2) Turn fabric at end of stitching. Position lace edge next to first row of hemstitching. Stitch slowly, making sure wing needle enters holes exactly on first line of stitching and straight needle pierces edge of lace.

How to Hemstitch an Insert Using a Single-Wing Needle & Special-Purpose Presser Foot

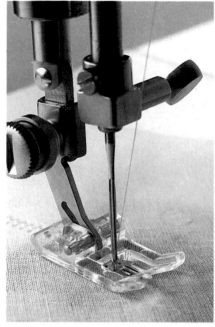

1) Set machine for zigzag stitch of medium width and length. Stitch a section of organdy fabric slightly larger than motif to be appliquéd; begin first row of stitching on bias grain, using single-wing needle and special-purpose foot.

2) Turn at end of row, keeping tip of needle in fabric. Stitch next row so needle pierces holes on one side of previous row with every other swing. Continue stitching in this manner until block is covered.

3) Place stabilizer under area of garment to be appliquéd. Straight-stitch appliqué to garment on outer edge of design, using embroidery hoop, if necessary, to keep fabric from puckering.

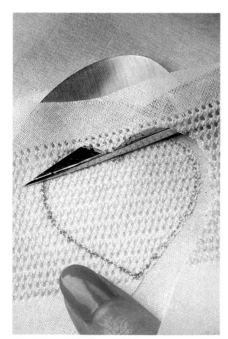

4) Cut excess appliqué fabric close to stitching line. Duckbill appliqué scissors help to cut close without cutting into stitches.

5) Stitch over previous stitching line and cut edge, using satin stitch. For extra emphasis, satin-stitch again, using a slightly wider stitch.

6) Remove stabilizer. Trim away fabric under hemstitched motif.

Even Feed™ Foot

There is no need to be timid about buying some of the beautiful, unusual fabrics available today. Pile fabrics, genuine or synthetic suede and leather, and quilted fabrics are among those that pose challenges at the sewing machine because they slip or stick to the presser foot. But the Even Feed foot (also called the walking foot) makes these special fabrics as easy to sew as muslin.

With an all-purpose presser foot, fabrics slip during machine stitching because the feed dogs grab only the lower layer. Meanwhile, the presser foot simply pushes the upper layer against the lower layer. For most fabrics, slippage of the upper layer against the lower layer is only slight and can be controlled by pins. But even a small amount of slippage is obvious on a striped or plaid fabric that requires matching.

With feed teeth of its own, the Even Feed foot synchronizes the rate at which upper and lower layers of fabric feed under the needle. Sticky fabrics are not held back by the presser foot, because it "walks." Stripes that start out matched remain matched the entire length of a seam. Multiple layers can be machine-quilted without puckers, and stretchy velours stay together for smooth seaming.

Pin-tuck Foot & Twin Needle

Pin tucks are one of the most versatile of all decorative effects. They look tailored when sewn vertically on a crisp shirt, demure across the yoke of a soft blouse, and ethnic when alternated with rows of colorful embroidery. They can also serve a practical purpose as pleats in a garment, holding in fullness.

Traditionally, pin tucks are formed by stitching very near a folded edge, but an easier method is to use a pin-tuck foot and a twin needle. The two needle threads share one bobbin thread, which pulls the fabric up between the rows of stitching. Twin-needle pin tucks are always even because the two rows of stitching are exactly parallel. The grooves under the pin-tuck foot keep multiple pin tucks the same distance apart.

Twin needles vary in size and are numbered, first, according to the distance (in millimeters) between the needles and, second, by the size of the needles. For example, a 2.0/80 twin needle indicates that size 80 needles are spaced 2 mm apart.

Consult your owner's manual or dealer about pin-tuck feet for your machine. They may come in more than one size. The narrower the grooves, the finer the pin tucks will be. Use a larger-grooved foot for pin tucks in bulkier fabrics. For stitching pin tucks,

choose the twin needle size that most closely corresponds to the spacing of the grooves.

Twin-needle pin tucks require two spools of thread on top. To prevent the threads from tangling, place the spools so they unwind in opposite directions — the left spool to unwind from behind, the right one to unwind from the front. Increasing upper tension slightly results in a more pronounced pin tuck.

To add decorative pin tucks to a garment, sew them into your fabric before you cut out the pattern. For closely spaced tucks, guide the previous tuck down one of the grooves in the pin-tuck foot. Experiment with spacing by using different grooves. To leave space for embroidery between tucks, use the edge of the presser foot as a guide. Work all pin tucks in the same direction to avoid distorting the fabric.

Gathering Foot

Feminine is always in fashion, both in home decorating and apparel. That often means gathers and ruffles. You may think of gathers and ruffles as a tedious task, involving sewing two or three rows of basting stitches, drawing them up, and adjusting the fullness evenly. Gathering yards of ruffles this traditional way can take hours, but there is an easier and faster alternative.

A gathering foot is ideal for creating ruffles. You cannot adjust the gathers after stitching is completed, however, so the foot is not meant to gather a specific amount of fabric to fit another section, such as a sleeve to a cuff. Four factors determine how much fullness will be produced:

- Fabric — Lightweight, fine fabrics gather more than heavier, more dense fabrics.

- Stitch length — The longer the stitch, the more fullness will be drawn into each stitch.

- Tension — The tighter the tension on the machine, the fuller the gathers will be.

- Machine operator — For even gathering, let the machine feed the fabric; do not hold it back.

Experiment with strips of the fabric you will use for your project. Place fabric under the gathering foot and begin sewing. The foot does the work! Try different stitch lengths and tension settings until you achieve the fullness desired, and then record the machine settings used.

Ann Hesse Price is a freelance sewing writer based in Seattle. Her work appears regularly in Sew News *magazine.*

Using Special Accessories

Even Feed foot. Match stripes or plaids at beginning of seamline. Even Feed foot will keep them matched as you stitch seam.

Pin-tuck foot and twin needle. Tighten tension slightly. Stitch, with right side of fabric up. Place first tuck under channel of pin-tuck presser foot; determine distance from first tuck by channel selection. Stitch additional tucks.

Gathering foot. Set stitch length for long stitches; the longer the stitch, the greater the fullness. Tighten tension. Hold index finger behind presser foot while stitching. Fabric piles up against finger. Release finger, and repeat.

Computerized & Mechanical Sewing Machines: What Are the Differences?

by Gale Grigg Hazen

Today the question of which sewing machine to purchase is complicated by whether to choose a computerized or a mechanical model. A computerized machine generally is promoted as the higher-quality choice — but what, really, are the differences?

Keep in mind when you compare machines that the most important thing any sewing machine must do is join a seam with strong, uniform results. When you go for a demonstration, sew on all machines yourself to discover how each one works for you.

Both computerized and mechanical machines offer a wide array of features and options. The features will vary from one brand to another. An important consideration in buying a new machine is stitch or function selection. After all, the stitches — what types, how many there are, and how easy they are to select and to use — are what sewing is all about.

Stitch Length & Width

Computerized and mechanical sewing machines control stitch length and width in different ways. On computerized sewing machines, a minicomputer uses either a small stepmotor or a linear servomotor to control the movement of the needle and the feed dogs. With stepmotors, the amount the needle and feed dogs move is defined in steps. Some machines have many steps that allow for very fine adjustments to stitch width and length; others have fewer, larger steps, so stitches cannot be as finely tuned. Computerized sewing machines with linear servomotors, on the other hand, are not restricted or defined by steps. Like mechanical machines, they allow an infinite number of stitch length and width combinations.

Most computerized machines automatically choose the "right" length and width combination for you when you select a stitch. The simplicity of pushing a button that chooses for you can be very handy. But overriding a preset stitch width or length may be easy, difficult, or impossible, depending on the model.

A mechanical machine uses levers and gears to control the movement of the needle and feed dogs, so it is possible to get an infinite number of stitch length and width combinations. This allows for more precise sewing, but usually requires a more complicated set-up procedure, often an ordered series of steps.

Stitch Pattern Selection

Computerized sewing machines are able to offer the widest selection of stitch patterns. Their memory can store a great number of designs in a small space. The menu of choices for special stitches is virtually endless.

The selection of a stitch pattern on a computerized sewing machine involves the push of a button or programming in a specific number of stitches. For more complicated tasks like writing words (which involves stringing separate patterns together) or repeating patterns, their built-in memory makes it possible to program the entire sequence all at once. Many computerized machines can do one motif or a series or combinations of motifs, as well as mirror images of patterns. Some can elongate the patterns or be programmed to stop after stitching one motif in a pattern. Sewing machines vary in their procedure for setting up these more complicated pattern selections, with some procedures being difficult and others quite easy. When considering a machine for purchase, see how clear the instructions are by checking the manual.

A mechanical sewing machine relies on knobs or levers to make a stitch selection, so relatively few patterns are built into the machine. A few models require separate cams to extend the variety of stitches available. Patterns must be set up and completed one at a time. These limitations make mechanical sewing machines less convenient than their computerized cousins for creative crafts that rely on extensive use of decorative stitch patterns.

Buttonholes

Making buttonholes has always been the most complicated procedure on a sewing machine. Computerized sewing machines can execute identical buttonholes. Some computerized machines have a buttonhole foot that measures the length of the button, creating the same length for each row, or leg, of buttonhole stitches; others count the stitches to establish the length of the buttonhole. Some computerized machines have the additional advantage of stitching both rows, or legs, of the buttonhole in the same direction, rather than forward and back, for more even stitching. Also, you

may be able to adjust the space between the rows of stitches and the density of the stitches to customize the appearance of the buttonhole. Differences in nap and the thickness of fabric layers can affect the uniformity of a series of buttonholes. It is important to be sure there is an override system on computerized sewing machines for making buttonholes on difficult fabric or with difficult placement.

Mechanical machines require the fabric to be turned, or one or more knobs to be manipulated, to create a buttonhole. The length and density of stitches on a group of mechanically made buttonholes seldom are consistent and accurate. There are now special feet with visual guides for precise buttonhole lengths. Also, there are buttonhole attachments that can be used in place of the buttonhole function on mechanical sewing machines. Check with your dealer for details.

Reminders & Warnings

One special advantage of computerized sewing machines is their ability to provide reminders of options, as well as warnings about possible problems.

Most home sewers do not take advantage of all the feet and attachments that come with their machine. The proper foot for the stitch you select can make or break your project. Some computerized sewing machines automatically specify the proper choice of foot when you select a stitch; some also warn you about other things, like if a twin needle is not appropriate, or if you are about to run out of bobbin thread.

Features & Options

Needle Stop Up/Down. An option that is offered on some electronic sewing machines (both computerized and mechanical machines can also be electronic) is control of the position in which the needle stops, either up or down, when you stop sewing. This is a useful feature, for example, when you are changing stitching direction frequently in a piece of fabric; whenever you stop, the needle remains in the fabric, ready to pivot. Or, if you are stitching a lot of seams, select the up position of the needle, and you can pull your work free of the machine at the end of each seam.

Variable Needle Position. Many mechanical and a few computerized sewing machines have the option to move the needle to sew anywhere from center to left to right in the general-purpose or zigzag needle plate opening. Moving the needle rather than the fabric is helpful for maintaining control when topstitching and edgestitching, and is also the preferred method for tapering a line of satin stitching.

Speed Control. A traditional foot control slows sewing speed by cutting power to the motor. This is why the needle will not pierce heavy fabrics at slow speeds. An electronic motor drive system controls speed, using resistors to slow the motor while maintaining full power. Some mechanical and all computerized sewing machines have this electronic speed control system, which allows you greater control at both low and high speeds for more accurate sewing.

Directional Stitching. Some electronic models have directional stitching, which enables you to stitch "sideways." A square patch can be stitched without pivoting or repositioning the fabric.

Repairs

Repairing microchips used in computer boards is not possible in many cases, so computer chips for sewing machines are replaced rather than repaired. If a chip is going to fail, it will do so in the first few weeks or months. Your warranty will generally cover the repair. After this initial period, the life of a computerized sewing machine is relatively unlimited.

If the computerized sewing machine has a stepmotor, it can also require repair. It is inexpensive, but the labor necessary to replace it varies greatly.

Conclusions

The choice of a computerized or a mechanical sewing machine depends on how you sew and where your creative emphasis lies. If you use a straight stitch primarily for projects such as quilting or garment construction, the options on a top-of-the-line computerized sewing machine may be more than you need. If you use your machine for crafts or decorative clothing, the wide selection of stitches and ease of using them on a computerized sewing machine are very much to your advantage. What computerized machines really do best are patterns — single motifs as well as repeats and combinations.

To get the most out of any sewing machine, you need expert guidance on how to use it. Check out where, when, how, and by whom you will be taught to use the features on the machine you are considering buying. This is especially important with a computerized machine; the sequence for setting up and using its memory features must be followed precisely, and you will need careful instructions to do it correctly.

Gale Grigg Hazen, lecturer and teacher, owns a private sewing school called The Sewing Place *in Campbell, California. She is author of* An Owner's Guide to Sewing Machines and Overlocks *and* Sew Sane.

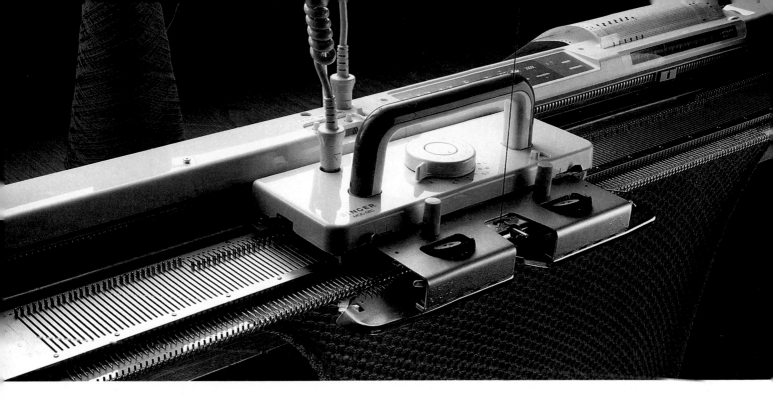

Electronic Knitting Machines

by Susan Guagliumi

Electronic models are the new kids on the knitting machine block. Many of the craft and needlework magazines have presented them as advanced machines for experienced knitters. However, a good case can be made for electronics for beginners, as well.

Knitting techniques are basically the same on all machines. Although an electronic knitting machine may look more complex, garment pieces are shaped by increasing and decreasing stitches, just as they are on any other machine. Unless you opt to install a motor drive, the carriage is moved by hand, just as on a punchcard model.

Electronic machines have a definite advantage over other knitting machines in terms of speed, flexibility, and creative application. And with good instruction, they are no more difficult to learn.

How Electronic Knitting Machines Work

Generally speaking, electronic knitting machines contain microcomputers that respond to the reflection, penetration, or absence of light on design sheets that are fed into the machine. You may use the design sheets that come with the machine, or you may draw your own original knitting patterns on gridded mylar using a special pencil. In either case, each square in the grid represents a single stitch. The knitting machine's microcomputer "reads" the pattern, using a beam of light. As the beam reads each square in the grid, the machine responds by knitting the corresponding color or kind of stitch.

Easy Repeat Designs

Knitting designs for punchcard machines are limited to 12, 24, or 40-stitch repeats, and to smaller designs that can be repeated within those formats. Electronic knitting machines allow you to decide how many stitches to include in a repeat; most can easily knit designs up to 60 stitches wide, without restriction. Although you can knit an endless variety of patterns on a punchcard knitting machine, you often have to compromise original designs to accommodate the machine's capabilities. For example, a classic 15-stitch snowflake motif would have to be altered by subtracting detail in order to fit a 12-stitch punchcard repeat, but it could be knitted exactly on an electronic machine.

An electronic machine also lets you increase or decrease the space between repeating motifs or use only a portion of a design. It lets you dictate the width of a motif simply by setting a dial or pressing a button.

On a punchcard machine, an entire pattern must be punched to knit a panel of fabric. On an electronic machine, just a few stitches or a few rows need to be programmed; they can then be repeated up and down or back and forth to knit a panel. Making patterns is thus much faster on an electronic knitting machine.

Custom Designing

Because stitches are generally wider than they are long, the "squares" on a mylar design grid are actually rectangles rather than squares. They are proportioned so what you draw is what you knit.

Many designs can be drawn freehand on the mylar sheets, without squaring off the edges or totally filling in each square. Unless you draw a small, detailed design, the machine automatically determines the edges of the design shapes from your sketch. With space for 150 rows of a pattern, it is easy to personalize sweaters with signatures, children's drawings, a company logo — virtually anything you can draw.

You can also create designs for an electronic knitting machine using a photocopied image. This is useful, for example, to knit a sweater to coordinate with a skirt made of patterned fabric. Photocopy the pattern from the skirt fabric, enlarging or reducing the size to suit your sweater design. Then lay a gridded mylar sheet over it and photocopy the two together. What you have now is a paper copy of the mylar pattern. You need only to trace this onto a blank mylar, squaring off the edges for small, detailed designs, and your finished design sheet is ready to feed into the machine.

Electronic knitting machines can repeat designs or isolate them anywhere on the knitting bed. And, even after a design has been fed into the machine and you have decided its placement on the bed, you can vary the pattern at the touch of a button, whenever and as often as you like. Push-button convenience allows you to use individual patterns in a variety of ways, and to alter them during the course of knitting.

Built-in Versatility

Most electronics have basic features like color and directional reversal. A color reverser allows you to switch pattern and background colors without rethreading the carriage. A directional reverser enables you to have a design face either left or right. Being able to control the direction in which a design faces is especially helpful when it comes to knitting words and letters, because you can draw them exactly as they should read, rather than in reverse, as you would on a punchcard.

Other useful features of electronic knitting machines are vertical and horizontal expansion. The machine can read each square of a design as either two rows or two stitches. When these features are used indi-

vidually, vertical expansion stretches designs lengthwise, and horizontal expansion makes them twice as wide. When the two are used together, designs are proportionately doubled. This is an easy way to enlarge a design motif. In addition, horizontal expansion allows you to knit on every other needle without having to redraw your designs — great for use with heavier yarns. There is also a button that makes any design suitable for knitting in double jacquard.

Horizontal and vertical mirror images of your designs can be produced at the touch of a button on an electronic knitting machine. This is a real time-saver. You only need to draw a half butterfly or a quarter circle, for example, then press the appropriate button to knit a complete motif.

The newest computerized knitting machines and accessories make it possible to produce motifs 200 stitches wide and 1000 rows long — a significant improvement over punchcard machines. They can read designs with three or more colors in a row, extract and enlarge portions of designs, and automatically combine several designs to form new ones. Electronics allow you to work with or without mylar sheets. You can store your original designs on memory cards or floppy discs, or buy patterns on either cards or discs if you are not interested in designing your own. Initially, there is more to learn about the patterning mechanism, but you will not outgrow an electronic knitting machine as you progress from beginning to expert skills.

What to Look For

Whether you are a beginning or an experienced machine-knitter, the new electronic models are worth a close look. For any machine you buy, be sure the features you value either are built into the machine or can be added later as accessory purchases. All electronics now on the market are standard-gauge machines — they will not handle bulky yarns well.

Learn all you can about your machine. Find out whether there is a knitting club you can join or a schedule of advanced classes from which to choose. Lessons and support are important with any knitting machine, but they are even more important with an electronic machine, so you can take full advantage of its versatility.

Susan Guagliumi is a knitting consultant for The Singer Company and a frequent author and contributing editor of Threads *magazine.*

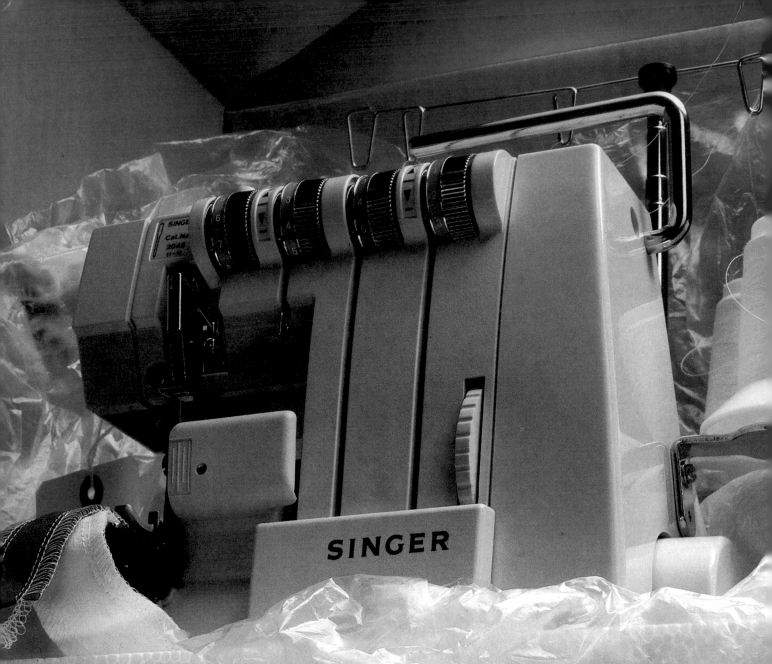

Is Your Serger Still in the Box?

by Sue Green

If you answer "yes," don't hang your head in shame — many of the sergers sold today are still in their original package. Why have so many of us not let this little beast out of the box?

Until I purchased my serger, nothing in the sewing product line intimidated me. Taking my new serger out of the box gave me the same feelings I had when I first tried to drive a car with a clutch. As with the car, I had a few jerky starts with my serger the first time I used it. So will you.

But, practice will make perfect! I truly believe that the only person who dashes home and immediately becomes a serging expert is the same person who can put together a child's swing set — the deluxe model — in 15 minutes flat.

It is normal to be intimidated by this odd-looking little sewing machine. It's okay. You are not alone. And you can master it!

The Decision to Buy

When you decided you needed a serger, you took a big first step toward helping yourself become a more proficient and professional seamstress.

Walking into the store, you were prepared with at least a hundred questions to ask the salesperson about this new kind of sewing machine. As the salesperson demonstrated the serger, you witnessed the machine make a seam that took half as long and looked twice as good as what you could do on your conventional sewing machine. The salesperson quickly maneuvered the fabric through the serger, convincing you that anyone could sew with one. "This is for me!" you thought. As you wrote the check, your mind was racing with ideas for a closet full of new clothes.

Carefully, you placed the little machine in the trunk of your car. Before you reached the parking lot exit, though, you began to have second thoughts. Will I really use it that much? Can I learn to operate it? Should I have spent all that money? These feelings are normal.

Excuses, Excuses

My serger sat on the dining room table on display for almost a week. When the family started to ask silly questions like, "When are you going to make something with it?" I promptly put it back into the box and stashed it out of sight.

Returning my serger to its box was a major mistake for me. Maybe if it had been left out as a visual reminder, I would have used it sooner. On the bright side, moving the box around to different areas of the sewing room gave me a great feeling of control. The manufacturer had thoughtfully built handles into the box to make this task easier.

One of the ploys I used to convince myself I needed a serger was the fact that I could make $20 T-shirts for the kids in ten minutes. Unfortunately, I made the mistake of telling my oldest son about the ten-minute T-shirt.

Eventually, someone in the family is going to make the Ten-Minute T-Shirt Request. You must be prepared to handle this request with conviction. Simply say, "I didn't buy that model. My serger takes much longer." They do not need to know, just yet, that with a little practice, your serger can be trained to make a T-shirt in ten minutes also.

The Decision to Sew

Eventually, the day will arrive when you and the serger are all alone. The time has come to take it out of its box.

If you are like me, you will carefully remove the packing material and lift the serger out of the box. Then you will realize that everything the salesperson told you about the serger has left your brain. Momentary panic sets in. "What do I do next?"

My advice, as a survivor of the serger unboxing experience, is to adopt a positive attitude and open the owner's manual.

The Owner's Manual

Position yourself in front of the serger and open the manual at the beginning. This book will become your best friend, in time.

Familiarize yourself with the parts of the machine. Every manual has a page that shows the name and location of each part in the machine. At first glance, it will seem they have used another language to describe sewing machine parts. Sergers do have parts that are different from parts on conventional sewing machines. You will need to learn the differences between them.

As you read the manual, strange phrases will appear. The following are some of the more common ones.

Serger loopers take the place of bobbins in the machine. Loopers are mechanical arms that carry the thread back and forth at the needle to create stitches. Sergers do not have bobbins. The biggest plus about this feature is that there is no chance of running out of bobbin thread. You can see how much thread you have left at all times.

The loopers and needles on a serger form their stitches around a small metal prong on the needle plate. This stitch finger, or stitch prong, prevents the overedge stitches from pulling tight around the edge of the fabric and rolling the edge of the seam allowance. On some models or brands of sergers, you have to change the needle plate to one with a larger stitch finger, or prong, to change the width of the stitch.

The bite adjustment on a serger refers to the stitch width setting. The more fabric the knife blades bite off, the narrower the serge stitch.

Sergers can use large cones of thread. These cones have a large opening at the base. A cone adapter, or cone holder, is placed on the spool pin to fit inside this large opening and prevent the cone from moving around on the spool pin.

Most sergers are supplied with several spool adapters or caps. These adapters are used on conventional spools of thread to help them feed evenly.

Tail chain, sometimes called after stitches, refers to the stitches left at the back of the presser foot when you remove the fabric from the machine.

Rolled hem stitch (1) is very similar to the stitch most often used as a finish for the edges of table napkins. It is called many other names, too, such as a curling stitch, fold-over stitch, felling stitch, roll stitch, narrow edge stitch, roll-over stitch, and lapping stitch.

Flatlock stitch (2) is used for joining two pieces of fabric together with the serger stitches showing on the outside of the garments. This stitch can be used for decorative or utility serging. It closely resembles the seam stitches used on ready-to-wear sweatshirts.

Overedging (3) refers to the finishing of a seam allowance only. Some machines can do this using only two threads. Overedging alone with two threads will not make a secure seam.

Overlocking (4) secures the seam and overedges the seam allowance at the same time. Overlocking is done with at least three threads.

As you learn to use the machine, these terms will become very familiar. After you become an accomplished serger sewer, you will easily add phrases like "I got my tail caught in the door!" "Put the knife down," "Pull up the antenna," "Left is loose, right is tight," and "Close the doors" to your new language.

Setting Up the Machine

Most sergers today come with small spools of thread on them that were used to test the stitch before the machine left the factory. Pull up the thread stand's telescoping pole to the highest point, and check to see if threads are wrapped around the spool pins or thread stand. Unwrap them if they are.

Open the doors and check to see if the threads are in their color-coded guides. If not, put them in. A quick-reference threading chart can be found on the inside of a door on the machine or at the beginning of the owner's manual.

Raise the presser foot and remove the test sample. The sample will be attached to the machine with a tail chain of stitches. Clip the tail chain close to the sample, leaving tail stitches on the serger. Plug in the power cord.

Threading the Serger

Threading a serger appears complicated at first, but really it is just different from a conventional sewing machine. A 3-thread serger has only one more thread than a conventional sewing machine. It's just that the loopers on a serger are in plain sight.

A serger will almost thread itself if you let it. Factories that make ready-to-wear garments do not shut down to rethread their sergers, and neither should you. Simply cut the old threads and tie on new colors; then pull the new color through the machine using the tail of the old one.

How to Thread a Serger Using the Tying-on Method

1) Clip threads just in front of the needles. (Your serger may only have one needle.)

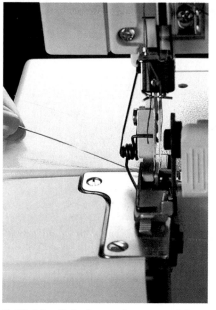

2) Hold tail chain, and run machine slowly until you have 3" to 4" (7.5 to 10 cm) of straight threads behind the presser foot. (A chain will not form because the needles are not threaded.)

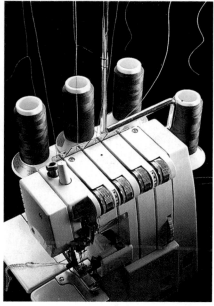

3) Cut threads close to spools on thread stand. Place new colors on stand. Tie new and old threads together. Clip threads 1" (2.5 cm) from knot; if you clip tails close to knot, threads may come untied.

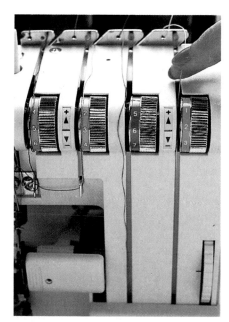

4) Remove threads from each tension dial by pulling above and below dial. Raise presser foot.

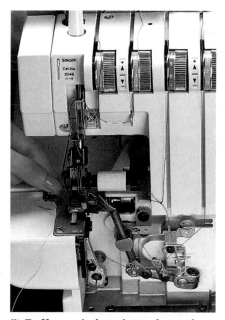

5) Pull one tied-on knot through machine, pulling gently on thread end from behind presser foot. If thread does not pull easily, check whether it is caught on thread guide or wrapped around thread stand. Pull other threads through machine, one at a time.

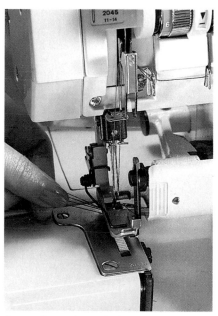

6) Replace threads in tension dials by pulling snugly between tension discs. Thread needles after cutting off knots. Bring all threads under and slightly to left of presser foot. Lower presser foot. Run machine slowly to form tail chain.

Trial Runs on Scraps

As you sew and cut on the serger, avoid pulling or tugging on the fabric. Do not fight the machine. Practice serging on scraps, and watch where the knife blades are and how they work.

The serger handles fabric differently from a conventional sewing machine. With a serger, it is not always necessary to raise the presser foot to start a seam — which can be a real time-saver. For thick or difficult fabrics, raising the presser foot slightly to place the fabric under the foot will help prevent the fabric layers from shifting. For most fabrics, though, raising the presser foot is a matter of personal taste. I have kept the habit from my conventional sewing, of raising the foot at the beginning of a serged seam.

A serger will even form stitches with no fabric in the machine. To end a seam, continue to sew after reaching the end of the fabric, until you have a tail chain 4" to 6" (10 to 15 cm) long. Clip the tail chain, leaving some on the fabric and some on the machine behind the presser foot.

Most sergers have a seam allowance gauge on the front door to help you determine where to place the fabric to sew the correct-size seam. As you gain experience, you may prefer using other "gauges" for measuring seams — a mark on the serger or the side of the presser foot.

The Not-So-Terrible Tensions

Tensions are the most misunderstood feature on the serger! The first step in understanding them is to remove the word "tension" from your vocabulary — it has such unpleasant associations, like tension headaches and hypertensions. I like to call serger tension dials "pattern changers" instead.

The function of the serger tension dial is to change the stitch pattern from basic seaming to flatlocking to rolled hemming. On a conventional sewing machine, we change the tension because there is something wrong with the stitch. On a serger, we change the tension because we want the machine to do a different stitch.

To understand how to use the tension dials, first you must understand how and where each thread is used to form the serged stitch. Refer to your owner's manual to locate the needle tension dials, upper looper dial, and lower looper dial. Mark them with a piece of tape, if necessary, to keep them straight.

Most sergers have color-coded tension dials and thread guides to help with the threading step. Thread the machine with colors of thread that match the color coding on the machine, so that you can see clearly what each one does. For example, if your machine uses yellow to code the threading for the lower looper, use yellow thread in the lower looper.

Practice turning the tension dials while sewing on a long scrap of fabric. With the machine running, slowly turn one dial at a time and look at the change it makes in the stitch. The tension dials were set at the factory, so be sure to write down the number of the original setting on each dial before you begin.

Ready to Sew

I have always prided myself on being an independent sewer — "independent," meaning, "I can do that without someone showing me!"

There are times, however, when it just does not pay to be independent. Eventually, you will teach yourself to be a proficient serger sewer. At the beginning, though, humble yourself and return to the dealer who sold you the machine. Take a lesson or two. An experienced professional can teach you tricks in ten minutes that could take you months to learn on your own.

As you work with your serger, your fear diminishes and you start to feel comfortable and confident. With practice and patience, you will begin to really enjoy your new serger. Soon you will say, "Why didn't I have this wonderful machine ten years ago?!"

For Further Reading:
Sewing with a Serger, Singer Sewing Reference Library®.

Sue Green is a nationally known author, lecturer, and teacher who travels the United States teaching serger sewing. She entertains her classes with a lighthearted approach to this technical subject. Sue lives with her cat, Simon, in the small town of Sebastopol in northern California.

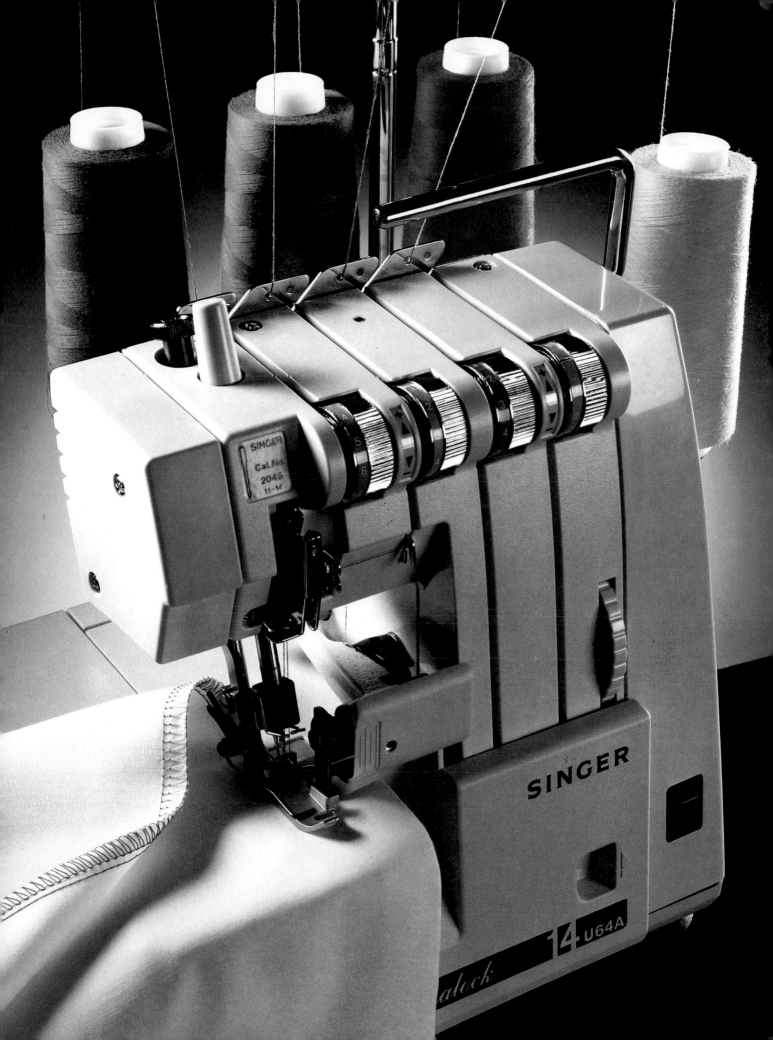

Surface Design

Surface Design and Embellishment

by Nancy Restuccia

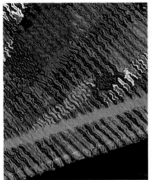

Why do you sew? Decades ago, the overwhelming answer was to save money. Today, most people sew to express their creativity: to make something unique, something enduring, something of quality.

It is not surprising, then, that the hottest trend in sewing today is surface design. Age-old techniques such as marbling, slashing, dyeing, piecing, and ruching are being adapted to create wearable expressions of individual style and personality.

A sampling of these techniques is presented in this article; other techniques are explained in greater detail in the articles that follow. Completed works by a handful of fiber artists are also pictured here. Instructions for making their garments are *not* included; rather, they are presented for inspiration in creating wearable art of your own.

Slashing

Slashing is a technique that enjoyed favor in Europe during the Renaissance. Contemporary fiber artist Tim Harding rediscovered the technique and has worked with it for years, adapting and updating it for a variety of colorful, textural effects. Essentially, it is a process of sandwiching and stitching together several layers of fabric, then cutting through some of them in spots to expose successive layers. When washed, dried, and brushed, the cut edges curl and fray to create a richly textured surface.

Harding's sophisticated artwear technique has been copied and popularized as "blooming" vests and T-tops, in which several full-size layers of fabric are slashed within a grid of squares. Slashing, though, may just as easily be done within a grid of rectangles or triangles, or between a series of lines. The fabrics may be layered as full-size pattern pieces, or bits and pieces may be sandwiched for interesting color variations. To be successful, tightly woven natural fiber (usually cotton) fabrics must be used.

How to Make Fabric "Bloom"

1) Cut six pieces of tightly woven 100% cotton according to pattern. Trim seam allowances off the four inner layers. Mark a grid of 1⅜" (3.5 cm) squares on top layer. Stack all six layers, matching seamlines; stitch together on marked lines.

2) Cut a ¼" (6 mm) slit in center of selected squares along diagonal, using seam ripper. Cut through any or all of the top five layers of fabric; do not cut through the backing layer. Clip from center to corners, using sharp scissors.

3) Wash and dry by machine to make the fabric "bloom." The more times you wash and dry it, the more fabric will bloom. If desired, brush surface with stiff brush to fray cut edges.

Contemporary fiber artist Tim Harding adapts Renaissance fabric slashing techniques to create his unique kimono-form greatcoats.

Photo credit: Collection of The Minneapolis Institute of Arts

Appliqué, Embroidery & Beading

Appliqué, embroidery, and beading are three surface design techniques in which something is applied on top of a base fabric. Often, these techniques are used in combination to produce striking visual and textural effects on the surface of a garment.

Traditionally, appliqué, embroidery, and beading have been done by hand. Today, stunning results may also be achieved using new machine sewing techniques and tools. Special presser feet are available for most sewing machines for satin stitching, darning, braiding, cording, and hemstitching. Many new threads specially designed for decorative stitching are available, such as ribbon threads, and silk and cotton embroidery threads. The decorative stitches built into your sewing machine — used creatively with interesting threads, cording, and fabric combinations — can yield attractive results.

When planning a sewing project that includes appliqué, embroidery, or beading, be sure to consider the compatibility of your materials. For example, don't use invisible nylon thread to sew an appliqué to linen; the high heat necessary to press the linen will melt the nylon thread. Don't use a noncolorfast ribbon or yarn to embroider a washable garment, or you'll have a streaky mess after the first laundering. Thinking ahead to such compatibility problems will save you time and trouble in the long run. Leather — such as used in artist Jan Faulkner-Wagoner's jacket, left — is an ideal fabric for appliqué, embroidery, and beading, since it requires washing so infrequently, never needs pressing, and does not ravel.

Leather artist Jan Faulkner-Wagoner uses machine appliqué, embroidery, beading, studding, eyelets, and buttons to create this "journal piece" — a garment that tells the story of her stay in Australia.

Piecing

Piecing has a rich history as a surface design technique. Traditionally, piecing was a way to use every scrap of fabric available — back when fabric was one of the most expensive of all personal possessions. Today, piecing has quite a different connotation, reflecting abundance of time, skill, and creativity.

Piecing is sewing small sections of fabric together to create larger ones. It may be done by hand or machine. Scraps can be combined to create geometric shapes or pictorial scenes, or they may be assembled randomly.

Several fabrics may be stacked and cut at the same time, using the new rotary cutting tools available today. This makes preparing the fabric for many traditional piecework patterns an easy job. Ethnic piecing traditions such as Seminole patchwork (page 54) also provide today's busy sewer with shortcut methods for creating pieced fabrics. A small pieced strip inserted diagonally into a skirt waistband or jacket front band, a miniature pieced "quilt" inserted into a man's tie, a randomly pieced yoke on a dress — these are just a few ways piecing may be used to make a garment unique.

A "prairie point" is another form of piecing. It is a triangularly folded piece of fabric sewn into a seam. Prairie points seem to float on the surface of a fabric. They can add interesting textural and color punctuation to a pieced garment or quilt.

How to Make a Prairie Point

Fold a strip of fabric in half lengthwise. Bring folded edges together at center. Press and trim ends to form a triangle. Stitch into seam. Folded edges may face either up or down.

Marit Lee Kucera combines strip piecing, Seminole patchwork, embroidery, prairie points, piping, tucking, and a variety of fabrics and textures in her fiber-art interpretation of winter in Minnesota.

Seminole Patchwork

Seminole patchwork has always been a machine tradition. In that, it differs from other piecing techniques. The Seminole and the Miccosukee Indians of Florida are known to have acquired hand-cranked sewing machines as early as the 1880s; but it was not until the 1930s and 1940s that the design possibilities of

their piecing tradition exploded. The simple strip-piecing techniques of these Florida Indians are some of the most adaptable for today's home sewers. Below are two of the many Seminole patchwork patterns you can make using this quick piecing technique.

How to Sew a Seminole Patchwork Strip (checkerboard)

1) Cut equal strips of two different fabrics on the straight grain. Stitch the strips together, using a ¼" (6 mm) seam allowance. Press seam to one side.

2) Cut the pieced fabric perpendicular to seam, into strips the same width as the original. A see-through ruler and rotary cutter are helpful for this.

3) Arrange strips in a checkerboard pattern. Stitch together, using a ¼" (6 mm) seam allowance; match center seams carefully. Press seams to one side.

How to Sew a Seminole Patchwork Strip (diagonal)

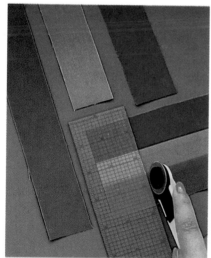

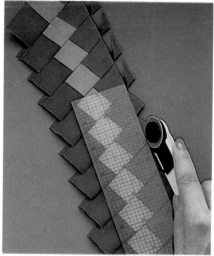

1) Cut equal strips of three different fabrics. Stitch together, press, and cut into strips as in steps 1 and 2, above.

2) Arrange strips so top of center stripe aligns with middle of center stripe on adjoining strip. Stitch, using ¼" (6 mm) seam allowances. Press seam allowances to one side.

3) Trim off points on raw edges to make the strip even.

Caryl Bryer Fallert uses dyeing, piecing, and pleating techniques to create this striking original suit design.

Pleating

Pleats are formed by folding and pressing fabric. Some very interesting effects may be achieved with pleating on striped fabrics. Artist Caryl Bryer Fallert created her own striped fabric by piecing gradations of colored fabric alternately with black. Then, she concealed the colored stripes within pressed pleats. Where the pleats are released at hip level, the colors blossom with the slightest movement.

For any striped fabric — whether you buy it or piece it yourself — the width of the stripes determines the width of the pleats. Experiment to decide which colors to show and which to hide within the pleats. Pleats may be released from a seam or held in position at one end with edgestitching.

Lightweight wools, cottons, silks, and linens will pleat sharply. Select crisp, firm fabrics for garments with pressed pleats. Also, check to see if stripes are on the straight grain before buying a fabric; pleats will not hang properly if they are not.

Dyeing & Painting

Myriad surface design possibilities exist within the realm of dyeing and painting. From puff paints to marbling, from tie-dyeing to batik — the color combinations, pattern choices, and techniques for applying dyes and paints to fabric are virtually endless. Dyes and paints can be spattered, brushed, sponged, stamped, and sprayed onto fabrics. Fabrics can be tied, folded, and treated with resist materials to create distinct patterns; they can be dipped whole or in part into dye and paint baths. Bleaches can be dropped, sprayed, and painted to selectively remove color.

Dyes and paints, as materials, differ in an essential way: With dyes, color is absorbed by the fiber and becomes a part of the fiber itself. With paints, the color sits on the surface of the fabric. Dyes penetrate; the color is essentially the same on the wrong side of a dyed fabric as on the right. The overall effect of dyes is soft; transitions from one area to another tend to blur and meld. With paints, there is a definite right and wrong side to your fabric. Paints generally allow for sharper definition than dyes, for more startling contrasts, and clearer-cut lines and shapes. These differences in the way the two materials behave can help you to decide whether a dye or a paint is appropriate for a given garment or to achieve a specific effect.

Resources

Despite the growing popularity of surface design and embellishment among sewers, many of the materials required may be difficult to find in some fabric stores. Craft stores, quilt stores, weavers' supply stores, and art supply stores may have what you need. Mail order may be your answer. The advertisements and classified sections in sewing, craft, and quilting magazines are great sources for patterns, instructions, books, and tools for surface design. *FIBERARTS, Handmade, Quilter's Newsletter Magazine, Sew News,* and *Threads* are magazines that advertise such products.

There are not many books available that deal with surface design and embellishment in a comprehensive way, but there are many fine publications that treat single topics. A few particularly good ones are listed below; there are others. You may not find these at your local bookstore. Check sewing, craft, and quilting stores, or look through sewing mail-order catalogs. Or, try your local art museum shop, or a college or university bookstore.

Surface design and embellishment is an exciting field of discovery for home sewers today. The techniques discussed on these few pages are by no means an exhaustive list; but they provide a good starting point for experimentation and creative expression.

For Further Reading:
Sewing for Style, Sewing Update No. 1, and *Sewing for Children,* Singer Sewing Reference Library®. *The Seminole Patchwork Book,* Bradkin. *Design and Sew It Yourself,* Ericson. *Heirloom Machine Quilting,* Hargrave. *Singer Instructions for Art Embroidery and Lace Work,* reprinted by Lacis. *Yvonne Porcella, A Colorful Book,* Porcella. *Decorative Dressmaking,* Thompson.

Nancy Restuccia is a Minneapolis-based freelance writer and desktop publisher, a former marketing manager and museum professional. She is hopelessly addicted to the art and craft of sewing.

Dyeing and painting are often confused because they are both materials and techniques. Here, dyes (the material) are painted (the technique) onto a fabric.

Yvonne Porcella combines the techniques of painting, piecing, quilting, and embellishing to create wearable as well as decorative art fashions, as shown at right.

Ruching Revived

by Sandra Ericson

Ruching. As we might expect, the term as well as the technique comes from the fashion-conscious French. Ruche — the French word for beehive — was originally used to refer to strips of gathered fabric, because they looked so much like the ridges on a straw beehive. Since the fifteenth century, when ruched trims were first documented on feminine dress, ruches have come to mean much more than simple gathered strips of fabric. Today, ruches also include pleated, folded, woven, braided, and feather-edged bands of fabric, lace, net, or ribbon.

The revival of ruching in the 1970s and 1980s reflects an appreciation of art-to-wear, valued for its evidence of true craft and creative expression. Our imaginations are the only limit to applying this technique in sewing.

Ruches may be either inset or applied to the fabric surface. When planning to use ruches, remember: whether they are inset or applied, they will add bulk and surface relief. Thus, ruches can emphasize underendowed areas of the body, or provide a fashion focus away from overendowed areas. Use ruches on shoulders, collars, and sleeves — areas that will not further define an already full figure.

Another factor to consider when planning to use ruching is fabric selection. Choose fabrics that enhance the technique itself. They should be strongly light-reflective — the play of light on the folded or gathered surfaces is part of the "show." Fabrics like taffeta, satin, metallics, or iridescents are quite dramatic. Transparent fabrics like organza, chiffons, or voiles used in certain areas of a gown can be quite sexy without being too revealing.

Ruched garment section (page 64) adds texture and surface interest to a simple gored knit dress, left.

Gathered inset ruche (page 62) accents the design line of a jacket.

Box-pleated applied ruche (pages 60 and 61) adds flair to the sleeve edge on an evening dress. Snail-shirred applied ruches are a softer alternative.

Tips for Sewing Ruches

Sew a test sample to determine the amount of fullness suitable for your fabric. Experiment to achieve the look you want.

Cut ruches on the bias if raveling or shaping around curves is a problem. Cutting on the bias also lessens the need for pressing.

Add a flat piece of fabric as a stabilizer to the wrong side of a ruched strip if shape of the garment might shift.

Triangle-tipped inset ruche (page 63) adds a sophisticated note to evening pants, right.

Applied Ruches

For applied ruches, strips of ruched fabric or
ribbon are attached to the surface of a garment. Most
often with this technique, the ruched strip is applied
by stitching down the middle. This allows the sides to lift
up, presenting an opportunity to finish the edges in a variety
of ways.

Edge finishes may include decorative stitching by machine or by hand;
"feathering," that is, raveling the edges for a fringe; or a rolled hem
stitched with a serger.

Applied ruched strips can add fullness to a hemline, emphasize a sleeve, or even
cover an entire evening gown for a stunning visual effect. Snail-shirred ruches, top
three above, add a soft scalloped effect to a garment. Box-pleated ruches, bottom two
above, can be embellished by joining pleats together with beading or embroidery.

How to Make a Snail-shirred Applied Ruche

1) Cut fabric strip on lengthwise grain to desired width and two to three times finished length. Finish edges as desired. Fold strip on true bias lines; press folds.

2) Stitch a continuous gathering line, following bias folds. Draw up threads to gather. Apply to garment, sewing by hand or by machine along gathering stitches.

How to Make a Box-pleated Applied Ruche

 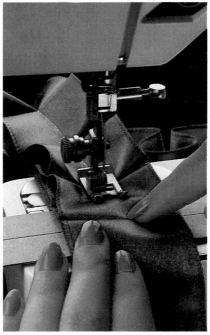 

1) Cut fabric strip on straight grain to the desired width and three times the finished length. Cut cardboard template the desired depth of each pleat and two times as wide as strip. Mark center line of template.

2) Finish edges of fabric strip as desired. Fold strip over template, forming pleat; finger press. Remove template and stitch along center of strip to secure pleat. Repeat to end of fabric strip.

3) Pinch opposite sides of each box pleat together. Tack at center of upper edge by hand or by machine. Stitch a bead at the center of each pleat when tacking, if desired.

Inset Ruches

Ruches may be inserted into a seamline to accent a design line on the pattern. Or, add your own design line to a garment by cutting a garment section apart and inserting a ruche.

Inset ruches may either be gathered or pleated. Gathered inset ruches may be gathered equally on both sides and inserted in a straight seamline, or unequally, to follow a curved seamline. Pleated inset ruches, such as triangle-tipped ruches, are inserted only in straight seams. Stabilize inset ruches with a lightweight backing fabric applied to the wrong side of the ruche, if necessary.

How to Adjust a Pattern for an Inset Ruche

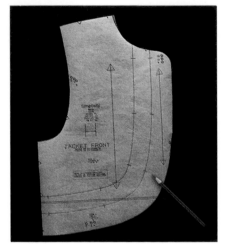

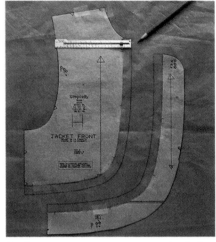

Add ruche centered on seamline. Draw new cutting lines (red) one-half the finished width of ruche from edge on both pattern pieces. Draw new seamlines (blue); transfer pattern markings.

Add ruche to garment section.
1) Mark desired finished width of ruche on pattern. Add markings for alignment. Draw a grainline on outer piece.

2) **Cut** pattern apart on marked design lines; add ⅝" (1.5 cm) seam allowances.

How to Sew a Gathered Inset Ruche

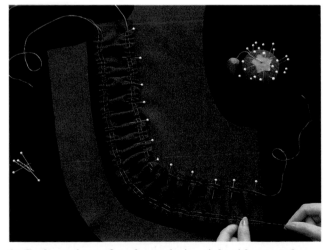

1) **Adjust** pattern, above. Cut out garment. Measure seamline where ruche will be inserted; on curved seamlines, measure longest edge. Cut fabric strip for ruche one and one-half to three times the length of seamline by the desired finished width plus 1¼" (3.2 cm) for seam allowances.

2) **Gather** edges of ruche and pin, right sides together, to fit garment edges. On curved ruches, gathers will be tighter on inside curve. Stitch to garment, gathered side up. Grade seam allowance of ruched strip before finishing edges. Press seam allowances toward unruched sections.

How to Sew a Triangle-tipped Inset Ruche

1) Adjust pattern, opposite. Cut out garment. Cut fabric strip for ruche five to six times the finished length by desired width plus ½" (1.3 cm) for seam allowances. Cut cardboard template one-half the width of strip plus ⅛" (3 mm) by two times the width of strip.

2) Finish edges of fabric strip by serging or zigzag stitching. Fold fabric strip over cardboard template and press into pleats; space pleats ¼" (6 mm) apart.

3) Fold each pleat again so corners meet in center; press. Continue to fold and press, forming a series of triangles.

4) Fold fabric between triangles to form narrow pleat, so each triangle overlaps partway over preceding one, covering raw edges. Press edges sharply. Tack invisibly along center back, catching underlayer only.

5) Finish seam allowances of garment. Pin ruche to garment, right sides together; match seamlines and align markings across ruche. [Ruche has ¼" (6 mm) seam allowances.] Stitch, ruche side up. Press seam allowances toward unruched sections.

Ruched Garment Sections

A commercial pattern may be adapted to create a garment with a ruched section, such as the dress pictured on page 58. Use this method for ruching an entire garment section, or just a portion of it. Depending on the pattern and the fabric, it may be necessary to stabilize the ruched area with a backing fabric, so the garment retains its shape when worn. A soft, lightweight fabric, such as chiffon or tricot, may be used for the stabilizer. For more body in the ruched area, use a firmer, crisp stabilizer, such as taffeta or organdy.

How to Ruche a Garment Section

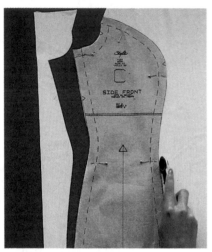

1) Cut fabric for stabilizer, if desired, from the section of pattern piece to be ruched.

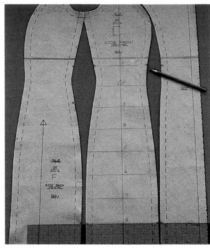

2) Mark where ruche begins and ends on pattern piece to be ruched, and on adjacent pieces. Extend grainline to length of pattern piece. Draw parallel lines 2" to 3" (5 to 7.5 cm) apart in area to be ruched. Number sections.

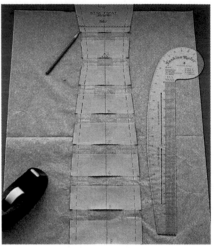

3) Draw grainline on tissue paper; lay pattern on top. Cut pattern on marked lines. Expand ruched section one and one-half to three times in length, distributing extra length evenly. Draw cutting lines and seamlines. Mark ends of ruched area.

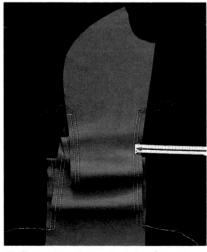

4) Cut out garment; transfer pattern markings. Stitch two rows of gathering stitches ¼" (6 mm) apart on edges to be ruched, with first row just inside seamline.

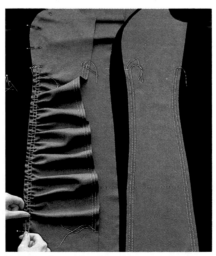

5) Match ruched section to garment section, pulling up gathers evenly and aligning markings; pin. Baste stabilizer, if used, to wrong side of ruched section. Stitch seams with ruched section up.

6) Trim seam allowances of ruched section. Finish seam allowances separately. Press seam allowances toward flat section.

Other Ruching Ideas

Once you have mastered ruching, let your imagination run wild. Try package decorations of ruched ribbon or crepe paper (very stitchable), ruched fabric jewelry, holiday ornaments, or Halloween costumes. Ruching is a show-stopper in large scale: think of a 45" (115 cm) piece of fabric as a strip to ruche. Do not limit your materials, either. You can ruche paper, nonwoven interfacings, cellophanes, nets, laces, meshes — anything that can be stitched. Try ruching several transparent layers together for an interesting effect.

Ruching also has wonderful possibilities for highlighting home interiors. Adding ruched borders and inserts to pillows, bedspreads, draperies, shower curtains, towels, slipcovers, and table linens is often easier than adding them to garments — the pieces are bigger, the seams are straighter, and fit is not so crucial. Home decorating projects are a good place to experiment with ruched designs.

With a little practice and imagination, you will be on your way to ruching like a pro. You will find yourself hunting for places to slip it into your sewing projects — encouraged by the thought that your creative effort and skill will make a big difference in the look and value of the finished garment.

For Further Reading:
Costumes in Detail, Bradfield. *Victorian Fashions and Costumes 1867-1898,* reprinted by Dover Publications. *The Art and Craft of Ribbonwork,* reprinted by Sandra Ericson. *Clothing Construction,* Mansfield and Lucas. *Decorative Dressmaking,* Thompson.

Sandra Ericson has taught fashion history and design at San Francisco City College since 1971. She also publishes The Art and Craft of Ribbonwork.

Marbling Fabrics

by LaVonne J. Horner

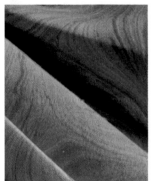

Marbling is the ancient art of decorating fabric or paper by floating pigments on a thickened water base, manipulating the pigments into a desired pattern, and transferring the pattern to fabric or paper. Probably its most familiar use was as endpapers in old books.

The tradition of marbling goes back to eighth-century Japan and the production of Suminagashi paper. The art of marbling expanded to Persia and Turkey, finally reaching Europe in the fifteenth century. Like many handicrafts, marbling declined in popularity during the Industrial Revolution. Contemporary artists are rediscovering the craft today, and finding new ways to use it.

Marbling allows you to "paint" on fabric, even if you cannot draw. You do not need an extensive knowledge of color and design to produce beautiful results. It does not have to take a lot of space. It can be done using readily available, inexpensive materials. And the result of your efforts is unique.

Marbling is a printing process. Each print is one-of-a-kind. It can be done using paints, inks, dyes — virtually anything that transfers color to fabric. It can work with almost any fabric, too, but usually the best results are achieved with natural fibers. Either white or colored fabrics can be used. However, the fabric color affects the results, since the coloring agents are very transparent. Texture is important, too; the smoother the surface of the fabric, the sharper the design.

To marble fabric, float drops of color on a thickened liquid, stir them with a stick or comb to create the marbled pattern, and then lay the pretreated fabric on top to transfer the color. Rinse, dry, and heat-set, and the fabric is ready to be included in your next sewing project.

For simplicity, start with a small project, such as napkins. Use 100%-cotton fabric and airbrush medium, a liquid paint packaged in squeeze bottles. Once you become proficient using these materials, you may want to experiment with larger pieces of fabric, other fibers, and different coloring agents. Acrylic tube paints and Turkish inks marble well, for example, and smooth silks accept the marbled color beautifully.

Sources (partial listing):

Cerulean Blue, Ltd., P.O. Box 21168, Seattle, WA 98111-3168; *Pro Chemical & Dye, Inc.* P.O. Box 14, Somerset, MA 02726; *Creative Fibers,* 5416 Penn Ave. S., Minneapolis, MN 55419; *Dharma Trading Co.,* P.O. Box 916, San Rafael, CA 94915

LaVonne J. Horner teaches marbling, weaving, needlepoint, and quilting throughout the country. Her passion for marbling stems from her commitment to uniqueness and fiber/fabric experimentation, as well as a fascination with color and design.

Supplies

100%-cotton fabric (must fit into pan without folding).

Pan of nonporous material (such as a disposable aluminum pan) about 1½" to 3" (3.8 to 7.5 cm) deep and width and length larger than fabric to be marbled.

Small pan for testing how paints spread.

Carrageenan, a nontoxic emulsifier made from seaweed (available as a powder from art and craft supply stores, weavers' supply stores, and by mail order).

Blender for mixing carrageenan with water.

Airbrush medium in your choice of colors (available from art and craft supply stores, weavers' supply stores, and by mail order).

Orange stick or stylus and a hair pick for drawing through the paint.

Newspaper for cleaning base between prints.

Ammonium alum (available from drugstores, art and craft supply stores, weavers' supply stores, and by mail order) to prepare fabric prior to marbling.

Basin or bucket for soaking fabric; rubber gloves.

Night-Before Preparation

Fabric:

Wear rubber gloves when mixing ammonium alum.

Mix 4 to 6 tablespoons (60 to 90 ml) ammonium alum in 1 gallon (3.78 l) water in bucket.

Soak fabric in ammonium alum for 20 minutes, stirring once; wring fabric.

Dry mediumweight to heavyweight fabric in clothes dryer. Line-dry fine cotton or silk; keep fabric wrinkle-free to avoid ammonium alum marks from uneven drying.

Press dry fabric with hot iron. Marble ammonium alum-treated fabric within one week. Wash out ammonium alum if fabric will not be marbled within one week.

Base:

Mix ½ to 1 level tablespoon (7.5 to 15 ml) powdered carrageenan in a blender full of warm water while agitating. Agitate 1 full minute.

Empty into pans. Mix more carrageenan as necessary to fill both large and small pans to depth of 1 inch (2.5 cm). Let stand overnight.

How to Marble Fabric

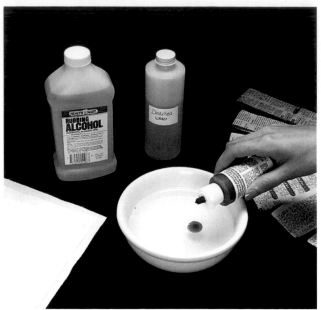

1) **Drop** paint on surface of carrageenan in small pan to test how well it floats. Drop carefully, taking care not to break surface of carrageenan. A drop should spread 1" to 3" (2.5 to 7.5 cm). If a color does not float well, add distilled water to paint, one drop at a time. If a color does not spread well, add rubbing alcohol to paint, one drop at a time. Test again.

2) **Drop** paints on carrageenan in large pan. Draw stylus slowly back and forth across surface, at about 1" (2.5 cm) intervals. Take care not to create bubbles by drawing too fast.

3) **Draw** stylus up and down across surface again at 1" (2.5 cm) intervals, perpendicular to first pattern.

4) Draw hair pick across surface. Hair pick may be drawn in any pattern you like, but usually perpendicular to direction of last drawing works best.

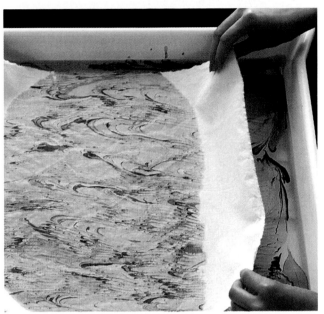

5) Lay ammonium alum-treated fabric on base, lowering middle first, then easing ends down so no air gets caught between fabric and pigment. Pattern will adhere almost immediately to natural fiber fabrics. For blends, pat lightly to ensure printing.

6) Pull fabric over edge of pan, leaving as much base as possible. Rinse under running water to remove excess paint and base. If colors rinse out significantly, increase proportion of ammonium alum when preparing fabric. The minerals in water affect this, so judge by trial and error. Wring fabric and line dry.

7) Clean base before marbling another piece of fabric, using newspaper folded to width of tray. Scrape paint off surface by pulling newspaper across base. Repeat marbling process for remaining fabric, beginning with step 2. Drop paints in same sequence to color-coordinate fabric. Age marbled fabric two weeks. Set color by drying in hot dryer 30 minutes.

Dyeing Fabrics

by Debra Millard Lunn

Have you ever tried to match a color in fabric? Or tried to find fabric in a color that was not in style at the time? How about finding a sequence of colors, ranging from light to dark or making a smooth transition from one color to another?

If you have tried, you know how difficult it can be. Perhaps dyeing your own fabric is the answer. The range of colors possible in hand-dyed fabrics far surpasses what is available commercially. Using just five colors of dye — the primaries (red, yellow, and blue) plus black and brown — you can dye literally thousands of colors. You can create fabric colors that are intense or subdued, pale or dark. You can dye fabrics in a rainbow of colors and a wide range of neutrals. The possibilities are virtually endless.

There are many kinds of synthetic and natural dyes. For hand dyeing, I recommend a Procion® fiber-reactive dye. These are the dyes the textile and garment industries have been using since the 1950s. Procion dyes make a chemical bond with fabric, and thus are lightfast and washfast. Procion dyes produce a transparent color. This means the dye penetrates the fabric rather than sitting on top. This also means that the weave structure of the fabric is visible and there is no change in the feel of the fabric.

Procion dyes can be used on all natural fibers, from cotton to silk to rayon. They do not work on synthetic fabrics or blends containing synthetics. These dyes work in a warm-water dye bath — no heating or boiling is required, just warm tap water. And, compared to other dyes, fiber-reactive dyes are relatively safe to use.

Although these dyes are some of the safest available for hand dyeing, remember that dyes are chemicals and that dyeing is chemistry. Avoid direct skin contact with the dyes and the setting chemicals by wearing long pants and a long-sleeved shirt, and by protecting your hands with rubber gloves. Avoid inhaling the dye powders; always use a face mask. A pollen mask is adequate unless you do a lot of dyeing; then, a professional respirator is recommended. (Recently, liquid Procion dyes have been introduced. While these do not pose the hazard of breathing airborne dye particles, they are somewhat less stable and less colorfast than powdered Procion dyes.)

Never eat, drink, or smoke while dyeing so you do not ingest any dye powder, or solution. Do not dye in your kitchen or any other eating area. Do not dye if you are pregnant. Keep dyes, as you would any chemicals, out of the reach of children. And use your dyeing equipment only for dyeing. Never use your measuring spoons and cups for cooking, too! If you follow these instructions and use common sense, dyeing can be safe.

The equipment needed for dyeing is simple — buckets, spoons, cups, rubber gloves, and a face mask — and can be found at your local grocery, hardware, or drugstore.

Fabrics should be of all-natural fibers with no surface finish. Refer to the end of the fabric bolt to see if a fabric has been treated, for example, with a permanent-press finish. It is possible to dye a fabric with a permanent-press finish; however, it will take two to three times the amount of dye to produce a particular color, and it may be more difficult to dye it evenly.

Two of the chemicals needed for dyeing are available from your grocery store: salt (either iodized or non-iodized) and water softener. Dyes, washing soda (also known as soda ash), and synthrapol (a special detergent) are available from weavers' supply stores or by mail order. Do not be tempted to buy washing soda from the grocery store. This kind of washing soda contains bleach and would bleach out the color you are trying to put in!

The easiest technique to use with fiber-reactive dyes is immersion dyeing: fabric is put into the dye pot and comes out one color. You can modify the technique by blocking part of the fabric from dye penetration by folding and tying it. By folding in different ways and using rubber bands or cords, you can create striped, checked, and starburst patterns with tie-dyeing.

Guidelines for Dyeing

Two basic aspects to consider when mixing colors are: hue (pure color) and value (lightness or darkness of a color). Tints are lighter values; shades are darker values. It is possible to dye any color, but the way you achieve each depends on whether it is a hue, a tint, or a shade. Test the hue on a fabric scrap when mixing the dye concentrate, page 74.

	Red	Red-Violet	Violet	Blue-Violet	Blue
Red Dye	6 tsp. (30 ml)	4½ tsp. (22.5 ml)	3 tsp. (15 ml)	1½ tsp. (7.5 ml)	0
Blue Dye	0	1½ tsp. (7.5 ml)	3 tsp. (15 ml)	4½ tsp. (22.5 ml)	6 tsp. (30 ml)
	Blue	**Blue-Green**	**Green**	**Yellow-Green**	**Yellow**
Blue Dye	6 tsp. (30 ml)	3 tsp. (15 ml)	1 tsp. (5 ml)	¼ tsp. (1.25 ml)	0
Yellow Dye	0	3 tsp. (15 ml)	5 tsp. (25 ml)	5¾ tsp. (28.75 ml)	6 tsp. (30 ml)
	Yellow	**Yellow-Orange**	**Orange**	**Red-Orange**	**Red**
Yellow Dye	6 tsp. (30 ml)	5¾ tsp. (28.75 ml)	5 tsp. (25 ml)	3 tsp. (15 ml)	0
Red Dye	0	¼ tsp. (1.25 ml)	1 tsp. (5 ml)	3 tsp. (15 ml)	6 tsp. (30 ml)

Hues are created by mixing the primary colors — red, blue, and yellow — in various proportions. The concept is simple: red plus yellow makes orange; red plus blue makes violet; and blue plus yellow makes green. Vary the proportions, and you get greenish blues, reddish oranges, and so on.

For most colors, a total of six teaspoons (30 ml) of dye powder per yard (.95 m) of fabric gives a strong hue. Because the primary colors have different strengths, the proportion of each color you need to mix to get a specific hue will vary. Yellow, for example, tends to be weaker than blue, so mixing three teaspoons (15 ml) of each will not give a true green; rather, more of a blue-green. The chart at left shows the proportions for mixing secondary colors, such as violet, and tertiary colors, such as red-violet and blue-violet. To create other hues, experiment to find the proper amounts to mix, always maintaining the six-teaspoon (30-ml) total per yard (.95 m) of fabric.

When mixing two hues to produce a third hue, you can generally tell what the third hue will be by dipping a scrap of fabric into the concentrated dye mixture, as in step 2, page 74.

Tints are achieved by decreasing the amount of dye powder in a dye bath. For a medium tint, use three teaspoons (15 ml) of dye powder per yard (.95 m) of fabric; for a light tint, try one teaspoon (5 ml) per yard (.95 m). With few exceptions, the value (the lightness or darkness of a color) of your dyed fabric is determined by how much dye powder you use, not by how long the fabric sits in the dye bath. Removing fabric from the dye bath early will only result in a fabric that is less lightfast and washfast. To dye a series of tints, use half the amount of dye for each piece of fabric. For example, to make four fabrics from true blue to light blue, mix four dye baths: the first using 6 teaspoons (30 ml) of dye, the second using 3 teaspoons (15 ml), the third using 1½ teaspoons (7.5 ml), and the fourth using ¾ teaspoon (3.75 ml).

Shades are dyed by adding black or brown to a hue. Blacks and browns are very strong colors; it does not take much of them to darken a hue. Use a total of 6 teaspoons (30 ml) of dye powder per yard (.95 m) of fabric; for example, ¼ teaspoon (1.25 ml) of brown plus 5¾ teaspoons (28.75 ml) of yellow. Experiment with proportions to achieve a particular shade.

Gray shades are achieved by adding black dye to a hue.

Earth shades are achieved by adding brown dye to a hue.

Night-Before Preparation

Wash fabric in synthrapol to remove sizing and to preshrink.

Supplies for dyeing 1 yard (.95 m) of cotton fabric

1 yard (.95 m) 100%-cotton fabric, with no surface finish

Synthrapol, a special detergent (available from weavers' supply stores, and by mail order — see "Sources" for partial listing of suppliers, page 76)

Procion® fiber-reactive dyes in red, blue, yellow, black, and brown for entire spectrum of possible colors (available from weavers' supply stores, and by mail order — see "Sources" for partial listing of suppliers, page 76)

¼ cup (59 ml) washing soda, also called soda ash (available from weavers' supply stores, and by mail order — see "Sources" for partial listing of suppliers; page 76.) Do not use grocery-store variety.

Plastic or enamel bucket, 3-gallon (11.4 l) capacity or larger

Set of measuring spoons, set of measuring cups, plastic or wooden mixing spoons

Rubber gloves

Face mask (available from hardware, drug, or dime store)

1 cup (237 ml) salt, either iodized or non-iodized

1 to 2 tablespoons (15 to 30 ml) water softener, if you have hard water

Rubber bands or nylon cord, if tie-dyeing

How to Dye 1 Yard of Cotton Fabric (immersion method)

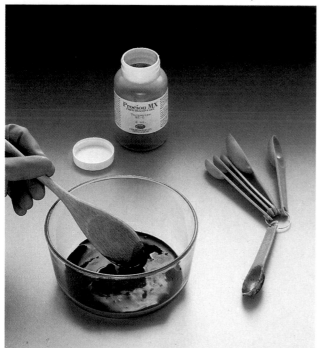

1) Mix dye powder with a little hot tap water to make a smooth paste (see chart, page 72, for quantity of powder). Add 1 cup (237 ml) warm water gradually, stirring until dye is dissolved.

2) Test hue by dipping wet fabric scrap into dye concentrate. Test will be somewhat darker than final color, because fabric is still wet and dye concentrate is darker than final dye bath. You may need to adjust the hue by adding a little more of one of the original dye colors (see pages 72 and 73).

3) Fill dye pot with 2 gallons (7.6 l) hot tap water. Add 1 cup (237 ml) salt and stir until dissolved. Stir in 1 to 2 tablespoons (15 to 30 ml) water softener for hard water. Stir in dissolved dye.

4) Add clean, thoroughly wet fabric to dye bath. Wearing rubber gloves, stir with your hands for 30 minutes; keep fabric submerged. Do not allow fabric to bunch up or to float above surface.

5) Dissolve ¼ cup (59 ml) washing soda in 1 to 2 cups (237 to 473 ml) hot water and add to dye bath. Do not pour washing soda solution directly onto fabric. Stir briefly, making sure all fabric stays submerged. Dye fabric 1 hour longer, stirring every 10 minutes.

6) Wash fabric in hot water, using synthrapol. Dry in clothes dryer at hottest temperature for 30 minutes. Press.

Tie-Dyeing

It is possible to immerse a piece of fabric in a dye bath, yet not dye it a solid color, using resist techniques. Resist techniques are methods of blocking parts of the fabric from contact with the dye. In batik, for example, wax is used to resist dye penetration. Tie-dyeing is perhaps the easiest and most familiar resist technique. Rubber bands, cords, and strings are used to block dye from penetrating the fabric. Popular in the 1960s, tie-dyeing is enjoying a resurgence today — updated by more intricate patterns, contemporary colors, and some interesting applications, including socks and tights.

Tie-dyeing involves folding, twisting, or scrunching fabric, then tightly tying off sections. Innumerable combinations of color and pattern are possible, depending on how fabric is folded and how it is tied. Tie-dyed fabric may be immersed in successive dye baths for a multicolored effect. With some dyes, the various component colors penetrate fabric at different rates, resulting in a multicolored halo effect (starburst, opposite).

Folding the fabric in preparation for tying works best if the fabric is damp. Experiment with the techniques on these pages, using small pieces of fabric. For stripes and checks, use a ¼-yard (.25-m) square of fabric. For the starburst effect, use a ½-yard (.50-m) fabric rectangle. After folding and tying, immerse the fabric bundle in a dye bath prepared according to the directions on the preceding page. Once you have mastered these methods of folding and tying, invent and experiment with other methods. When you're done, you may want to sew your swatches together to make a unique quilt, or incorporate them into a garment as a decorative panel, a yoke, or a pocket facing.

By applying these tying techniques and color-mixing principles, you can dye fabric in any pattern, color, or range of colors imaginable. Practice using the three primary colors: red, blue, and yellow. Then add black and brown to create shades. Experiment! The real fun starts when you mix dyes to create a beautiful new color, then develop sequences of tints and shades using that color as your starting point. Or, create two new colors, and dye fabric to make a smooth transition between them. Then introduce pattern. The combinations are endless — and so is the fun in creating them!

For Further Reading:
Synthetic Dyes for Natural Fibers, Knutsen. *A Quilter's Guide to Fabric Dyeing*, Millard. *Surface Design for Fabric*, Proctor and Lew.

Sources (partial listing):
Dyes and chemicals: *Cerulean Blue, Ltd.*, P.O. Box 21168, Seattle, WA 98111-3168; *Pro Chemical & Dye, Inc.*, P.O. Box 14, Somerset, MA 02726; *FABDEC*, 3553 Old Post Rd., San Angelo, TX 76904; *Creative Fibers*, 5416 Penn Ave. S., Minneapolis, MN 55419. Fabrics: *Testfabrics, Inc.*, P.O. Box 240, Middlesex, NJ 08846; *Debra Millard Lunn*, 1225 Garfield St., Denver, CO 80206.

Debra Millard Lunn is a fabric artist, author, teacher, and lecturer. Her quilts, using hand-dyed fabrics and computer-drawn patterns, have been exhibited nationally and abroad. She also sells hand-dyed fabrics through her own mail-order business.

How to Make Three Tie-Dye Patterns

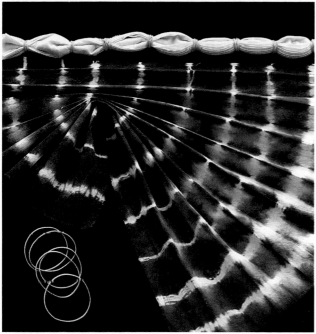

Stripes. Fold damp fabric into pleats about 1" (2.5 cm) wide. Wrap rubber bands around pleated fabric, spacing closely for narrow stripes, farther apart for wide stripes. Dye as on pages 74 and 75.

Starburst. Bunch fabric into tight ball. Wrap tightly with nylon cord (you should not be able to get your fingers underneath cord). Tie ends to secure. Dye as on pages 74 and 75. A halo effect occurs when blue dye penetrates fibers farther than red.

Two-color plaid. 1) Fold damp fabric into pleats about 2" (5 cm) wide. Fold pleated strip accordion-style, ending with a square bundle. Wrap nylon cord tightly around bundle, as if tying a package, wrapping several times in each direction. Dye as on pages 74 and 75.

2) Dampen dyed fabric. Re-fold into pleats; offset fold lines slightly from original ones. Fold and wrap as in step 1, left. Dye with second color, as on pages 74 and 75.

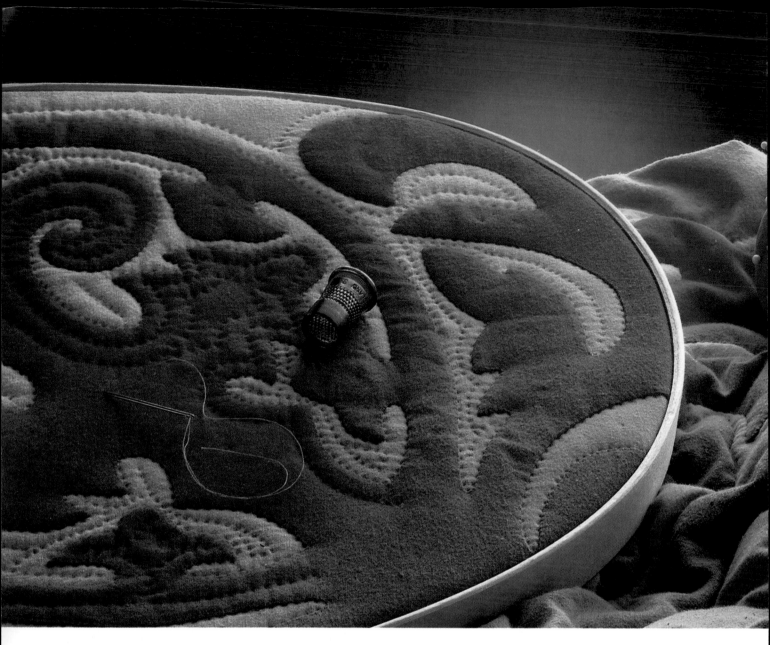

Hand Appliqué: A Quilting Tradition

by Patricia Cox

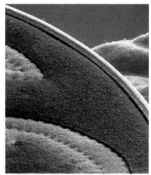

Appliqué quilting is often perceived to be a tedious, time-consuming craft. It does take time; but the time is amply rewarded. You can create any shape or form you desire within the limits of the technique. It can be realistic or abstract; the lines can be curved or straight. In a pieced quilt, most designs are based on straight lines, but in appliqué, most of what you do uses curved lines. There is much more freedom in appliqué than in piecing, so you can express more ideas.

There are several different appliqué methods. In regular appliqué, several pieces are arranged to create a design; each piece lies directly on the background fabric, except for small areas where an edge of one piece might lie under another. In multilayered appliqué, several pieces lie one on top of the other, giving the design a somewhat three-dimensional look. In reverse appliqué, such as in the Hawaiian quilt above, the top layer of fabric is cut away to reveal either another layer under it, or the background fabric.

There are many distinct styles and traditions in appliqué quilting. Some of the earliest appliqué quilts made in America used the motifs printed on chintz fabric; the individual elements were cut out, rearranged, and appliquéd to create a new design. When printed

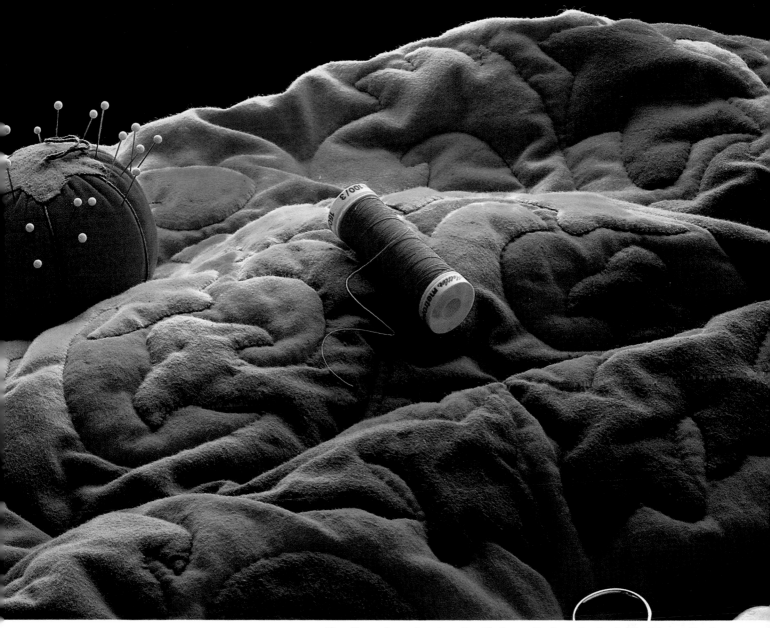

Hawaiian quilts are hand-appliquéd, then quilted to echo the shape of the appliqué.

chintzes became hard to get, plain fabrics were cut into shapes resembling the printed patterns and then appliquéd. Many very elaborate floral appliqué quilts were made in Baltimore — hence quilts in this style are called Baltimore quilts. After the Civil War, the popularity of intricate and elaborate appliqué designs for quilts waned, and simpler designs gained in favor.

Today, all types and styles of appliqué are being done. Pictorial quilts — ones depicting a scene — are popular, and there is a revival of interest in the Baltimore style. "Stained glass" appliqué is a recent innovation. Appliqué quilting techniques and styles are still evolving.

A number of distinct regional and ethnic appliqué quilting traditions are gaining in popularity today, as well. In the late 1800s, quilting was introduced in the Hawaiian islands by missionaries. The Hawaiians re-jected piecing techniques, and originated their own style of appliqué designs, based on local plants. A Hawaiian quilt consists of a single large appliqué cut from folded fabric, as you would cut paper "snow-flakes," and appliquéd to a contrasting fabric. This appliquéd top is then quilted to batting and backing fabric using "contour" quilting, echoing the pattern of the motif in rows of stitches ½" to ¾" (1.3 to 2 cm) apart.

About this same time, the Cuna Indians in the San Blas Islands off the coast of Panama were creating molas — multilayered appliqué motifs using both appliqué and reverse appliqué techniques. There are many similarities between molas and the work of the Hmong people, many of whom have immigrated to the United States in recent years. Both these ethnic traditions are very popular, and very collectible, today.

Appliqué Techniques

No matter what type of appliqué quilt top you choose to make — regular, multilayered, or reverse — you will need a needle and thread, pins, scissors, markers, a well-padded ironing board, and a steam iron. Beeswax and a thimble are optional, but very useful, additional notions. For Hawaiian and other large-motif quilts, you will also need shears. For quilts with motifs that are repeated, you will need to prepare templates for cutting pattern shapes.

Use a good-quality regular sewing thread. Match your thread to the color of the piece you are appliquéing. Work with a length of thread about 18" (46 cm) long. Longer lengths just get in your way and take too long to pull through the fabric, often creating small knots in the thread. And the more a thread is pulled through the fabric, the more it becomes fatigued, causing it to break. If your thread tends to tangle and break, try pulling it through beeswax.

Sew with the thinnest needle you can use comfortably. This may be a Sharp or a Between (a quilting needle). The length of the needle is less important than the thickness. I use a size 10 or 12 Between, but if that is too short for you, just be sure the needle is thin.

Templates may be cut from plastic or other materials. Cut templates without seam allowances. Add a scant ¼" (6 mm) seam allowance to each piece of fabric when you cut it out. At first, you may want to mark seam allowances before you cut; with practice, you will be able to judge the correct seam allowance by eye and eliminate the marking step.

When marking around templates onto your appliqué fabric, use a sandpaper board under the fabric to keep the fabric and template from slipping, and to make a darker impression with your marker. Make a sandpaper board by gluing a piece of very fine wet/dry sandpaper to a stiff piece of cardboard, plastic, or ¼" plywood.

The best stitch to use for appliqué is the blindstitch. It virtually disappears into the fabric. If you can learn to work the blindstitch both toward and away from yourself, it can be a big help. Some pieces are easier to sew in one direction than the other.

Take very small stitches when blindstitching. The smaller the stitch, the more control you have. Stitches ¹⁄₁₆" (1.5 mm) apart or less are recommended.

The heart is a classic design for teaching appliqué, because it includes techniques for stitching straight edges, curves, and both inside and outside corners. Careful placement of pins, minimum seam allowances, and the needle-rolling technique, combined with the blindstitch, allow you to sew smooth edges with invisible stitches without basting.

Patricia Cox is widely known as a teacher, writer, and artist in the world of quilts. Her articles, and pictures of her quilts, have appeared in many national quilting publications. She is a National Quilters Association Certified Teacher and Certified Judge.

How to Blindstitch a Heart Appliqué Using the Needle-Rolling Technique

1) Trace outline of design lightly on background fabric. Trace design on right side of appliqué fabric, with straight of grain running through center. Cut out appliqué with scant ¼" (6 mm) seam allowance.

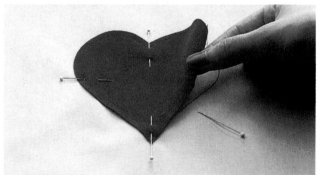

2) Match stitching line of appliqué to line drawn on background fabric; pin at top, bottom, and each side. Remove pin on straight edge; turn under seam allowance and repin through fold.

3) Tie knot at one end of thread. Bring threaded needle up through fabric from wrong side of appliqué slightly away from point at marked line. Knot will be hidden in fold.

4) Place heel of hand on background fabric and hold pinned fold with other hand. Holding fabric taut, use tip of needle to roll under seam allowance to make a smooth line.

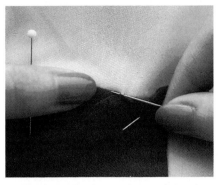

5) Put needle down through background fabric at edge of appliqué. Bring needle up into fold. Keep stitches small and needle parallel to edge of appliqué; pull thread snug. Blindstitch to pin.

6) Pin fold on curve ½" (1.3 cm) from last stitch. Roll under seam allowance and blindstitch, as in steps 4 and 5. Continue stitching to top of curve. Clip to point. Stitch to ½" (1.3 cm) of inside point.

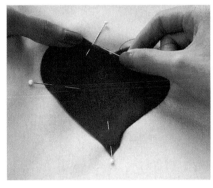

7) Pin folded edge just beyond clip. Roll under on marked line from pin to stitches, using a little tension from the needle; pull fabric taut so seam allowance will turn under smoothly.

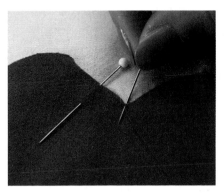

8) Stitch to point, rolling edge just beyond marked line at point; take two small overcast stitches. Stitch remaining curve in small segments.

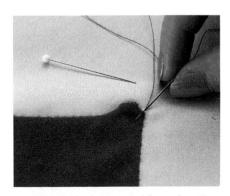

9) Blindstitch to outside point. Remove pin and take a small stitch. Fold seam allowance flat (90-degree angle) at the point. Take another stitch to secure point.

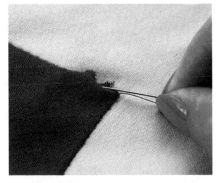

10) Use needle to pleat in seam allowance; this allows you to make a point half the width of the seam allowance. Tuck under remaining seam allowance; blindstitch.

11) End blindstitching by going over the same stitch three times on wrong side of background fabric under edge of appliqué. Run thread under appliqué; clip near surface.

Preserving Textile Works of Art

by Margaret A. Fikioris

Textile works of art are a product of loving care and exacting skill. Many hours go into their design and execution. Consider the number of hours devoted to making a contemporary quilt, for example. A hand-pieced quilt might take as much as 500 or 600 hours from start to finish. Even machine-pieced quilts can take 450 hours to complete. The sheer amount of time invested gives great value to these works of art in cloth.

Equal to time in giving a textile value is its emotional content. Fabrics, as decorative textiles or as costumes, mark important events and ceremonies in the lives of men and women. Often, these fabrics last beyond the lifetime of their creators and owners. The goal of textile conservation is to continue the lives of these fabrics.

Proper care is important at *all* stages in the life of a textile we want to preserve, from creation through old age. While it is obvious that old textiles require special handling, we rarely consider that new textiles require the same care if they are to look good when they are old.

Our natural inclination to touch fabric — to caress smooth silky floats or to rub fuzzy wool surfaces — is one of the greatest threats to the life of any textile. Each touch of the fingers can leave oil, grime, and dirt on the surface of a fabric, to become embedded within the fibers with the passage of time. Eventually, this weakens the fibers and may cause staining, discoloring, tearing, and other damage.

The best rule for preserving the life of a fabric is to avoid all unnecessary handling. Learn to avoid leaning on textiles as you work on them and to examine historic and treasured fabrics with the eye rather than the hand. If a textile has to be handled, then wash and dry hands thoroughly and often. Clean cotton gloves may help, but even they abrade fragile fabric surfaces.

Protect the surfaces of textiles to avoid frequent cleaning. Cover them with other fabrics or with acid-free tissue paper when you are not using them, to keep dust and dirt from settling. Cleaning is hard on textiles, and can shorten their lives considerably.

Light, heat, and humidity are also dangerous to fiber art. Keep textiles covered when not working on them, to prevent fading. Whether from sunlight or artificial light, damage to dyes and fibers is irreversible and is accelerated by heat, humidity, and pollution. Treat your valued textiles as allergic children — they are greatly sensitive to dust, smoke, and mold growth from a humid environment!

Do not smoke around textiles: nicotine turns fabrics yellow, tar and other by-products turn them dark gray, and all accelerate the fading of dyes and weakening of fibers. Keep all food products, including chewing gum and beverages, away from important textiles. Eating can leave crumbs, sugar, and oil residues that leave stains and attract insects.

When handling or constructing fiber art work, never wear jewelry. Pronged rings, dangling pendants or charms, and metal watchbands may snag or tear a fiber. Similarly, belt buckles, plastic tags, buttons, and even loose sleeves can cause permanent abrasion. Trim fingernails short, and avoid using hand lotions and bath oils.

When displaying or packing important textiles, do not use cellophane tape, masking tape, double-stick tape, staples, glue, pushpins, or tacks. All pens should be kept away; use pencils instead when writing or taking notes. Use cloth measuring tapes and smooth plastic rulers for taking measurements, never metal. Keep sharp-edged tools, such as scissors, mat knives, and seam rippers, on an adjacent table or inside trays or boxes. One slip can cause irreversible damage.

All textiles have fragile fibers that — like brittle bones — can be broken easily. Do not crush or fold textiles tightly when storing or transporting them, even for a short time. Keep them flat and evenly supported. When storing textiles, keep them safe from the damaging acids in ordinary paper and wood by using acid-free tissue, tubes, and boxes.

One of the most important considerations when working on, examining, or displaying a textile is support. Take particular care if you choose to hang a work of fiber art for display. Hanging produces great stress on a textile. The objective is to distribute the stress as widely as possible. For example, hang a quilt with hook and loop tape across the entire width of the top, not just in a few spots.

Cut a strip of 2" (5 cm) hook and loop tape the width of the quilt. Machine-stitch the loop side of the tape

to an equal length of 3" (9.5 cm) washed cotton webbing. Hand-stitch the webbing to the quilt, using a catchstitch around all sides of webbing; sew through all three layers of the quilt. Attach the hook side of the tape to a sealed wooden board with a staple gun.

For particularly heavy, old, or fragile fabrics, it is advisable to distribute the stress of hanging throughout the entire article. For a quilt, this entails hand-stitching a piece of new fabric across the entire back of the quilt and mounting it on a four-sided frame.

For more detailed information about hanging a quilt properly, as well as for sources of supplies, see the article by Patsy Orlofsky in *The Quilt Digest*, 1984, pages 58 to 69. For historic or particularly valuable textiles, contact a textile conservator or a conservation professional organization for advice or references.

With proper care and handling, the works of fiber art that you collect or create can last many generations. Each of us makes a difference in the continuation of the rich textile heritage that surrounds us.

Sources (partial listing):
Acid-free materials: *The Hollinger Corporation*, P.O. Box 8360, Fredricksburg, VA 22404. *Light Impressions*, 439 Monroe Ave., Rochester, NY 14607. *TALAS*, 213 W. 35th St., New York, NY 10001-1996. *University Products, Inc.*, P.O. Box 101, Holyoke, MA 01041.

Conservation Professional Organizations:
American Institute for Conservation of Historic and Artistic Works (AIC), 1400 16th St. N.W., Suite 340, Washington, DC 20036. *National Institute for the Conservation of Cultural Property (NIC)*, Arts and Industries Building, 2225, Smithsonian Institution, Washington, DC 20560. *Harper's Ferry Regional Textile Group*, Anderson House Museum, 2118 Massachusetts Ave. N.W., Washington, DC 20008. *Textile Conservation Group*, 1080 Park Ave., New York, NY 10128. *Washington Conservation Guild*, P.O. Box 23364, Washington, DC 20026. *International Institute for Conservation of Historic and Artistic Works (IIC)*, 6 Buckingham St., London WC2N 6 BA, England. *International Council of Museums (ICOM)*, Maison de L'UNESCO, 1 rue Miollis, 75732 Paris cedex 15, France. *International Centre for the Study of the Preservation and the Restoration of Cultural Property (ICCROM)*, 13 Via di San Michele, Rome 00153, Italy.

Margaret Fikioris is Textiles Conservator at the Henry Francis DuPont Winterthur Museum in Winterthur, Delaware. She teaches in the internationally recognized museum conservation training program sponsored jointly by the Winterthur Museum and the University of Delaware.

Wearable Fashions

Design Detail Inspiration

by Sandra Betzina

Give up being a slave to the pattern and you are free to incorporate design details from other patterns, fashion magazines, ready-to-wear, or pure imagination. Once you set this creative process in motion, making your own clothes moves swiftly into another realm. You are now free to imitate expensive ready-to-wear.

Design detail inspiration may be found in better department stores and boutiques. Garments and accessories with creative and interesting styling details command high prices. The price tag covers not only originality, but construction time as well. This is where the proficient home sewer has an advantage. Since high-fashion details rarely require additional fabric, adding these touches to a garment or accessory does not necessarily mean spending lots of money — more often, it is simply a matter of investing a little extra time. And the end result definitely justifies the effort: a unique garment that gets rave reviews and envious glances from friends.

Depending on where you live, beautiful styling may be found anywhere from the "designer section" of the city's best department store to the trendiest boutique in town. Or, turn to fashion magazines for inspiration. In addition to the readily available domestic *Vogue* and *Bazaar*, check out international fashion magazines; my particular favorites are *Italian Linea* and *Paris Vogue*.

When shopping, keep an eye out for anything that seems particularly well-made or unique. Look closely at pockets, collars, lapels, topstitching, plackets, waistbands, and hem finishes. To a salesclerk, you are admiring the workmanship. As a sewer, you are subconsciously measuring and planning the steps to incorporate this detail into your next garment.

Since rulers and measuring tapes do not create goodwill and may actually get you thrown out of the store, body parts must act as your measuring devices. Pocket width may be the distance of five outstretched fingers. Flap detailing may be the depth of one thumb. Back hem length may be longer than the front by one forefinger. Note carefully the placement of the design detail on the garment itself. How far is the detail above or below the armhole? Is it centered or closer to the side or front? How large are buttons — the size of a thumbnail or of the nail on your little finger?

Success in duplicating a design hinges upon detailed observation. After you have looked and felt your way around a garment that has particularly inspired you, run — do not walk! — to the nearest coffee shop to record your observations. Do not rely on your memory. Many great ideas have been lost while grocery shopping or driving the carpool. Always carry a notebook and pen in your purse to write down ideas for your next sewing project. A design idea notebook can be a lifelong treasure. Sometimes a design seen two years ago may be the perfect solution for customizing and creating additional interest for a current sewing project.

Design details need not be complicated to attract attention — sometimes they even simplify construction of a garment and save time. One of my favorites is to eliminate facings whenever possible by substituting contrasting trim. This accomplishes two things: it eliminates bulk, and it provides design interest.

Try trimming wool with suede or leather, summer-weight wovens like silk tweed or noile with linen, or cotton knits and wool jersey with a contrasting knit or ribbing. To ensure a smooth, ripple-less fit around curves, cut woven trim on the bias and cut knit trim on the crosswise grain. Suede and leather trim should be cut in the direction of greatest stretch. Synthetic suedes such as Ultrasuede®, Lamois™, and Caress™ lack grain and may be cut in any direction, since little stretch can be expected. Experiment on scrap fabric to get the desired effect.

Another simple design idea copied from ready-to-wear is the substitution of one large button for a series of buttons on a jacket. Choose the button carefully and it will become an accessory. Because large buttonholes are seldom attractive, substitute a fabric loop sewn into the seam for the buttonhole closing.

Another place to look for design detail inspiration might be right in your own closet. Look for a garment with a favorite pocket, waistband, yoke, cuff, or collar. Making a pattern of a design detail is a simple process. Perhaps the fastest way to make a pattern of the detail is to trace it with waxed paper and a tracing wheel. This gives you a pattern minus the seam allowances.

Normally, when copying a finished garment, 5/8" (1.5 cm) seam allowances are added. In my experi-

ence, adding and sewing a seam of ⅝" (1.5 cm) can result in a design detail that is slightly smaller than the original. For a more accurate copy, you may need to add up to ⅞" (2.2 cm) to cut edges, but stitch ⅝" (1.5 cm) seams. The amount to add to the cut edges will vary, depending on your tracing and cutting techniques, the size of the design detail, and the weight of the fabric. Of course, now is the perfect time to change the design detail slightly, if desired.

Some design details can be added without making a pattern. For an unusual pocket idea, try a series of three welt pocket openings spaced 1" (2.5 cm) apart with one long pocket behind all three. Finish only the bottom welt as a working pocket; sew the two upper pocket welts to the back pocket by a line of stitching in the ditch along each seam. This design detail is excellent on a linen, suede, or silk shirt.

Roll-up sleeves on a jacket can become a fashion accent by facing the sleeves in a contrasting or companion fabric.

Simple waistbands can be made more interesting by adding a fabric extension to one end of the waistband and securing it with a D-ring closure in leather or brass.

For a shirred waistband effect without the hassle of three or four rows of thin elastic inserted through casings, use 1" to 2" (2.5 to 5 cm) webbed elastic instead. While most elastics stretch or curl when stitched, almost no elasticity is lost by stitching through the webbed variety. To get the effect of several rows of thin elastic, thread the webbed elastic through one wide casing and stitch the fabric, elastic, and casing together along several equally spaced lines. The finished effect is a traditional shirred or ruched waistband, completed in considerably less time than numerous rows of thin elastic.

Sandra Betzina writes a syndicated sewing column and is the author of the textbook Power Sewing: New Ways to Make Fine Clothes Fast *and the instructional video* Power Sewing: Designer Details Made Easy.

How to Make a Pattern to Duplicate a Design Detail

1) Fold or draw grainline on waxed paper. Place paper over design detail, aligning grainlines. Pin to secure.

2) Trace around the finished edges of the design detail, using a tracing wheel.

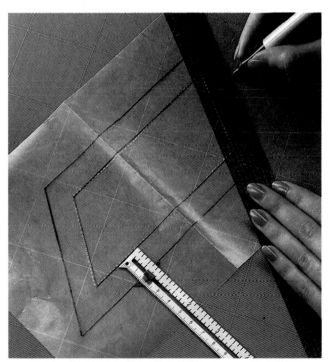

3) Remove paper from garment. If detail is symmetrical, fold along center line and true edges. Add ⅝" to ⅞" (1.5 to 2.2 cm) to all cut edges. Depending on your tracing and cutting techniques, the size of the design detail, and the weight of the fabric, the amount to add to the cut edges will vary slightly.

4) Cut design detail according to pattern. Stitch, using a ⅝" (1.5 cm) seam allowance.

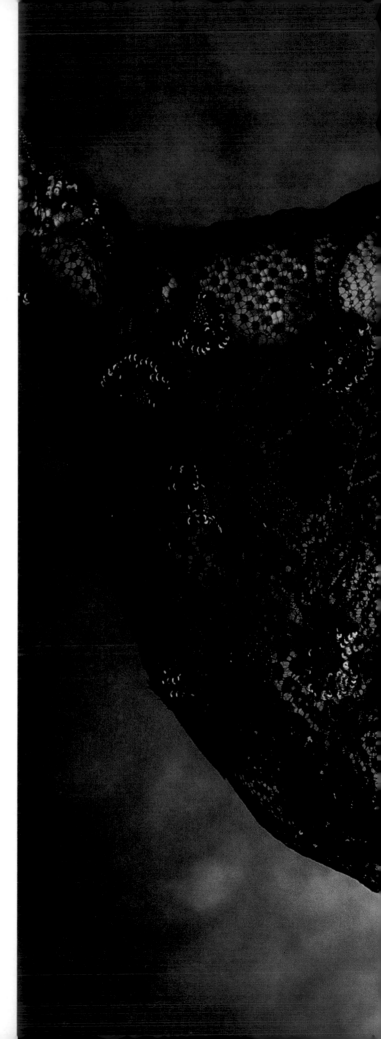

The Allure of Lace

by Susan Voigt-Reising

When major designers embrace a fabric or embellishment, others will not be far behind. In the case of lace, Jean-Paul Gaultier, Calvin Klein, and Geoffrey Beene, among others, have given us a sure sign that lace will be a fashion front-runner in the months ahead. From appliqués to entire suits, lace is everywhere in haute couture. And, thanks to the fashion "trickle-down" effect, it will also be found in the ready-to-wear lines in your local department stores, as well as on the shelves of your favorite fabric stores. Now, lace has more reason than ever to be included on your sewing shopping list.

The Lace Revolution

Though always a bridal staple and often an after-five favorite, lace shot to popularity for more casual attire more than four years ago. Spurred by female pop rock stars like Madonna and Cyndi Lauper, innerwear became outerwear, and lace bustiers and poufy crinolines strutted their way to new fashion heights.

By the fall of 1988, thanks to Beene, Gaultier, Klein, Christian Lacroix, and many other top designers, lace was everywhere: short and sweet as a slip of a dress and jacket; flirty and feminine as collars, ascots, and cuffs peeking out of man-tailored suits; sexy and sultry as overlays and off-the-shoulder bodices on evening wear; ornate and extraordinary as appliqué embellishments on everything from satin to leather.

A Lacy Future

What, then, is ahead? According to Doris Katz, manager of over-the-counter sales for lace manufacturer and importer Emil Katz, Inc., "Couture has always used laces, but never as much as now." In fact, "more" and "memorable" could be the bywords for lace today. "Designers are buying the most opulent lace they can get their hands on."

New York-based designer and lace master Ron LoVece sees this trend as an indication that "women want elegance, they want opulence . . . even though it's more expensive. They are looking for clothes that are going to be popular over time." And in LoVece's opinion, there is nothing more alluring, or timeless, than black lace.

Ribbon-trimmed
Chantilly

Sequined
and Beaded Chantilly

Soutache-trimmed
Chantilly

For home sewers, the current popularity of lace translates to an expanding selection of laces available in fabric stores and by mail order. The home sewer can choose from a variety of already-embellished laces, or can add embellishments herself. Sequins, beads, soutache, and ribbon are among the most sought-after accents for lace, with silvers and rainbow-hued iridescents dominating the spectrum of colors.

For ready-to-wear, Katz predicts lace's continued use as appliqués on a wide range of garments — on sweaters, especially — and as bustier dresses or short shirts with jackets. For cooler weather, she foresees lace joining forces with the fabric ultimate in opulence — velvet — plus the perennial lace-mates, satin and taffeta. LoVece looks for more lace collars and cuffs to soften tailored suits and usher them into evening, recommending the Irish Cluny variety for a crocheted, old-fashioned look.

Brides & Lace: A Perfect Marriage

Today's average bride is older and more sophisticated than her counterpart of two decades ago, and the new wide variety of colors and textures in specialty laces suits her perfectly.

Katz and LoVece agree in predicting that the look of bridal lace will lean to the soft, fluid, and romantic. LoVece, who designs the dramatic Marisa and the quietly elegant LoVece Ltd. bridal lines, chooses a very fine Chantilly lace to exemplify these qualities. He is quick to add, though, that the reembroidered richness of Alençon still reigns supreme in bridal. For those looking for something less formal — for example, a daytime wedding suit — LoVece sees cotton Venice lace, one of the few domestic laces, as a less-expensive, yet beautiful, alternative.

Overall, LoVece says, "The look, even in bridal, is becoming very, very sexy. We're doing very décolleté looks with a certain amount of illusion." Though a neckline may be high, see-through lace insets keep it interesting. Sleeves are very sheer, with a faint motif.

Don't Despair, Duplicate

With designer and ready-to-wear lace garments all around you for inspiration, and a multitude of beautiful new lace fabrics available in stores, all that remains for the home sewer is the creating.

Check the pattern books at your local fabric store for plenty of lacy ideas. And even if your pattern choice

Venice

Cluny

Chantilly

Alençon

does not list lace among its fabric options, think creatively. Why not take your cue from a favorite designer and add Chantilly lace sleeves to make that evening dress extra-special? Give that cardigan set character with a few well-placed lace appliqués in the same color as the sweater knit you choose. Make that day-into-evening blouse distinctive with a Cluny lace collar. Or create a body-hugging evening gown from one of the new stretch laces. Adapt and invent! Lace makes it especially easy because of its myriad looks and no-ravel nature. Whether you purchase your lace as an allover, trim, or appliqué, its uses are nearly limitless.

For fashion sewers looking for new ways to use lace, LoVece shared two of his own superquick ways to make the most of this feminine flirtation: To add color to a lacy bodice or appliqué, cut out the center of a flower motif and insert a satin rosebud in a color to contrast with the lace. To make a fashion-forward hair accessory or collar brightener, cut out a lace motif, back it with heavy tulle or crinoline and crush it. Secure it with a comb in the hair or pin it at the collar for a lovely evening accent. Add satin ribbons or a velvet bow for extra richness.

Whether you sew the subtly stunning, glitteringly glamorous, or something in between, follow designer inspiration — or your own fashion instincts — to add a little lace to your life.

Susan Voigt-Reising is assistant editor for Sew News *magazine and former associate producer of the fashion sewing television show "Make It Fashion."*

Tips for Sewing Lace

Use as few seams as possible. Choose a pattern with a simple design, and eliminate any unnecessary seams, such as straight center front or center back seams.

Study the lace design before you cut, to decide where to place seams and what technique to use to sew them. Because they are see-through, laces require seams that call as little attention to themselves as possible.

Wrap the toes of the presser foot with transparent tape, or cover the lace with tissue paper as you stitch, if the toes get caught in the lace while sewing. If the lace gets pulled down through the hole in the general-purpose or zigzag needle plate, put tissue paper under the fabric.

Mark pattern symbols that fall in an open space on the lace by placing a small piece of transparent tape on the wrong side of the fabric, and mark the symbol on the tape.

Large-Size Savvy

by Peggy Bendel

Fortunately, attitudes about large sizes have changed dramatically over the past ten years. Now if you wear a large size, there is no reason to feel like a fashion outcast. Regardless of what the tape measure says, you can wear whatever makes you look good and feel good. Not even horizontal stripes are taboo, if they work for you.

Updated Fashions Suit Your New Image

Today's large-size styles are geared toward a woman who enjoys following fashion trends and even setting the pace. Full-figured models project an attractive image in fashion shows, pantyhose commercials, trend-setting magazines, and pattern catalogs. Top designers, such as Calvin Klein, Oscar de la Renta, and Bill Blass, have recently extended their sizing into the high double digits.

Credit for large-size acceptance in the fashion industry belongs partially to advocates such as Nancye Radmin and Carol Shaw. Radmin founded The Forgotten Woman group of boutiques when she could not find desirable clothes following a post-pregnancy weight gain of 80 pounds (35 kg). She maintains, "Fashion is not a size. It's a sense of style." Shaw, editor of the magazine *BBW: Big, Beautiful Woman*, was inspired by her own large size to campaign for freedom of fashion choice. She says, "More than 30% of adult women wear size 16 and up. We used to be woefully neglected, but now we've come a long way."

The message is clear: You are as important as the woman who happens to weigh less, and it is time to dress the part. To improve your appearance from this updated point of view:

• Dress for the body you have now, not for the body you wish you had. Why postpone dressing attractively? Big can be beautiful; get rid of the guilt and develop a positive attitude.

• Try something new. If your wardrobe is dominated by timid neutrals, add touches of color such as a peach blouse for your gray suit. If you have been hiding under loose tunics, try a defined waistline.

• Make a fashion statement. You have the advantage of built-in presence: You can carry off wearable art, capes, jewel-encrusted laces, and eye-catching accessories. Be as dramatic or conservative as you like, but do show your style.

Patterns designed especially for larger sizes are available from several manufacturers

More Patterns in Your Size

For large-size sewers, it is especially easy to show your style today because pattern selection has never been greater. Most brands now extend Misses' patterns up to size 24, 46" (117 cm) bust, to give you the same up-to-date choices offered to others.

In addition, there are patterns specially designed for full figures. Burda offers patterns up to extra-large European size 60, 57½" (146 cm) bust. Great Fit Patterns specializes in sizes as large as 60, 64" (163 cm) bust. Simplicity recently revived the Women's size range up to 50, 54" (137 cm) bust, as has Vogue under the designation Misses' Large Sizes 14W to 30W, 36" to 52" (92 to 132 cm) bust. These sizes fit a larger bust cup and fuller body contours than Misses'.

Good Fit Is Essential

Not only can you find the styles you like in the size you need, but when you sew you can also customize the fit. This is the best favor you can do for your appearance, because good fit magically camouflages figure flaws. There are a number of steps you can take when you sew to ensure a more flattering fit:

• Select a larger pattern size if you usually add 2" (5 cm) or more to major areas of a pattern. If you add to the bust and midriff of Misses' patterns, switch to a Women's size. If you are sensitive about this, remember size is just a number, not a definition of beauty or a value judgment. The size you wear is your secret when you sew.

• Take advantage of multi-sized patterns with three or more sizes in one envelope. If you are one size on the top and another on the bottom, simply taper from one cutting line into another as you cut.

• Adjust bust darts for your figure. When multi-sized patterns provide a single dart, it is for the middle size only and should be fine-tuned for you. The fuller and rounder your bustline, the shorter and deeper bust darts should be. You might also angle the darts up to "lift" a sagging bustline. And darts for fuller bustlines should end 1½" to 2" (3.8 to 5 cm) away from the bust point, rather than the typical 1" to 1½" (2.5 to 3.8 cm) distance.

• Blend any adjustments. The more seams, darts, and similar details in a pattern, the better. If you have to let out seams or add to the pattern, you can distribute the amount you add among several areas rather than distorting the garment in one area.

• Construct an inside stay to prevent soft pleats, side-slant pockets, or gathers from bulging out. An inside stay is a flat piece of fabric — it may be muslin, two-way stretch fabric, or a lining fabric — sewn between the side seams as a foundation upon which the fashion fabric floats.

• Add other inner supports to your garments if you wish to conceal your true body shape, such as shoulder pads, interfacings, and underlinings (a lightweight fabric cut and sewn to each pattern piece and treated as one with the fashion fabric during construction).

• Avoid a tight fit. When you are fitting a pattern, first pin out design details such as tucks, gathers, and pleats; then fit the pattern with the necessary amount of ease. In general, a garment that skims the body is more elegant and flattering than a snug fit.

• Create figure-flattering optical illusions with minor alterations of design details. For example, you may change the style of pocket, size or placement of buttons, fullness of gathers, or direction of pleats.

For Further Reading:
The Perfect Fit, Singer Sewing Reference Library®.

Peggy Bendel, a contributing editor of Sew News, *has written numerous magazine articles and books on sewing-related topics.*

Couture Sleeves

by Roberta Carr

Sleeves are fashion. Sleeves offer endless opportunities for detailing. As we sit, talk, and gesture, they are there for the world to see, to examine, to admire.

Careful shaping and attention to detail in sleeves can make the difference between a professional and an obviously homemade look in a garment. Haute couture — high fashion — design and construction techniques contribute to a look that is extraordinary, rather than ordinary. Once you have mastered the basics of sleeve construction, you may want to move beyond the instructions in your pattern envelope and add one or more of the following couture details to your sewing repertoire.

Sleeves with Shaped Center Seams

A popular design detail this year is the two-piece sleeve, with a center seam running from cap point to wrist. In this variation on a traditional tailored sleeve, all of the ease has been incorporated into the seam. The result is a sleeve that sets into a garment beautifully, requiring only a minimum of shaping.

In order to retain the beautiful shape of this type of sleeve, first sew the seam and press it open over a curved edge — a ham or contoured pressing board — clipping where necessary. Then, apply interfacing. For a sleeve that will be lined, this might be Armo® wool (for a soft, cushioned seam), Sta-Shape® (for a sharp, rigid seam), or Hymo hair canvas (for a tailored seam), depending on the fabric of the garment. For an unlined sleeve, choose a bias strip cut from the fashion fabric or silk organza instead.

Topstitching the center seam gives this two-piece construction more body and adds decorative detail. If topstitching is not used, the interfacing should be attached by hand to the seam allowances only.

How to Interface a Sleeve with Shaped Center Seam

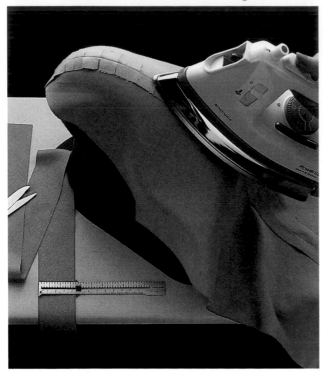

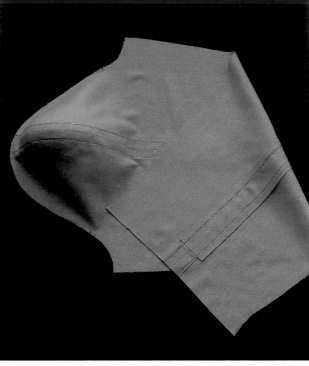

1) Cut interfacing on the bias 1¾" (4.5 cm) wide by finished length of sleeve. Stitch sleeve center seam. Press over a curved edge, clipping curves where necessary. Pin interfacing to sleeve, working from right side of sleeve.

2) Baste stitching lines through all thicknesses, with sleeve cap positioned on ham. Topstitch from hem edge on right side, ½" (3.8 cm) on each side of seam. If topstitching is eliminated, attach interfacing by hand to seam allowances only.

Bias-Cut Sleeves

The possibilities for couture details on sleeves are endless. Some of the most beautiful effects can be achieved by cutting sleeves on the bias. With designers like Christian La Croix giving bold plaids and checks a new arena in fashion this year, bias-cut sleeves also provide an easy solution to the problems inherent in matching plaids from garment body to sleeve.

Cutting sleeves on the bias changes how a sleeve will drape and is especially effective with softer fabrics. With a solid-colored fabric this is a subtle change. When

a stripe is used to create a chevron pattern, this design detail becomes the focal point of the garment.

Due to the nature of the grain, bias sleeves will hang thinner and longer than the same sleeve cut on the straight grain. Therefore, as with any bias garment, let sleeves hang after setting them in the garment for at least 24 hours before hemming them or applying cuffs. Be sure to hang the garment with shoulder pads inserted, preferably on a padded hanger, so the sleeves will hang naturally.

Tips for Cutting & Sewing on the Bias

Cut seam allowances 1½" (3.8 cm) wide. When fabric is cut on the bias, an explosion of fibers occurs along the cut, making the edge significantly longer than the original and intended length. If you stitch too close to the edge, your stitching line will be too long, resulting in a buckled and puckered seam. Pressing cannot correct this problem. The solution is to stitch bias seams 1½" (3.8 cm) from the cut edges, where the fibers are still intact.

Mark stitching line to ensure stitching a straight seam when sewing on the bias.

Use the smallest needle size possible and a stitch length of 12 to 15 stitches per inch (2.5 cm).

Stretch seam slightly as you sew, to prevent stitches from breaking when you wear garment.

Trim seam allowances after sewing seams, if required. It is not always necessary to trim bias seam allowances. On a skirt, for example, the extra fabric in the seam allowance provides additional support along the seamline.

Leave bias seam allowances unfinished; bias does not ravel.

How to Cut Sleeves on the Bias

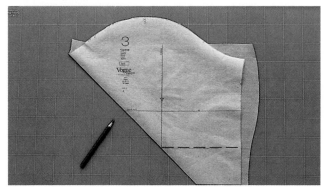

1) Fold pattern to form right angle at grainline marking. Mark new grainline along folded edge.

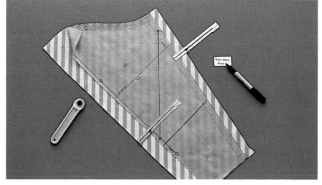

2) Place sleeve on single layer of fabric with new grainline on lengthwise grain of fabric; cap will point toward selvage. Cut, allowing 1½" (3.8 cm) seam allowances. Turn over pattern. Cut second sleeve with cap pointing toward opposite selvage.

How to Cut a Chevroned Bias Sleeve

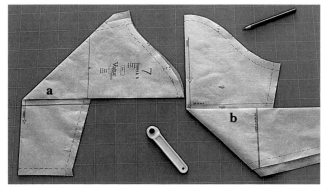

1) Fold pattern at center from shoulder dot to lower edge. For down-pointing chevron, fold pattern again from top to form right angle **(a)**; diagonal crease is new grainline. Or, for up-pointing chevron, fold pattern from bottom to create new grainline **(b)**. Cut pattern apart at center line.

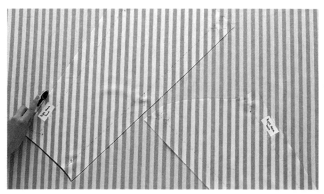

2) Place right sleeve front pattern on right side of single layer of striped fabric, with new grainline following stripe; cut with 1½" (3.8 cm) lengthwise seam allowances. Mark lengthwise stitching lines on wrong side of fabric. Mark each sleeve section on wrong side as it is cut.

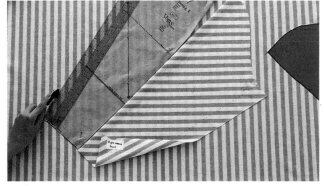

3) Place right sleeve front, right side up, on fabric; position next to right sleeve back pattern, matching stripes at a right angle to create a chevron at center *seamline*. Cut right sleeve back.

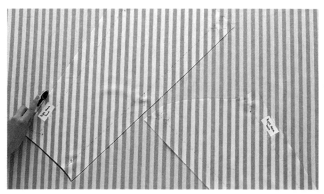

4) Cut front and back for left sleeve using right sleeve pieces as a pattern. Place right sides of fabric together, matching stripes.

Channel-stitched Cuffs

Channel-stitching is another popular design detail this year, appearing on plackets, yokes, collars, and cuffs. These closely spaced, parallel rows of stitches may look as if they were added to a completed garment as an afterthought, but for a truly couture look, they must be part of the construction process.

Shaping techniques — applying steam, heat, and pressure to add curve to flat fabric — are also crucial to achieving a couture finish for a garment. A cuff, for example, needs to wrap naturally around the wrist for a polished look. Shaping techniques assure that it will, by eliminating the excess facing and interfacing fabric that results when the three layers of a cuff are curved.

Couture sewing is an art. Practicing couture techniques requires a commitment to sharpen sewing skills beyond the basics, to accept new challenges, and to expand horizons. That commitment is amply rewarded in professional-looking garments and personal satisfaction.

Roberta C. Carr, known as "Bobbie," is the owner of The Fabric Carr, *a retail fabric store in Los Altos, California;* The Sewing Room *sewing school; and* Couture Summer Sewing Camp *in Carmel, California. She publishes* The Fabric Carr Sewing Tool Catalog, *and her writing has appeared in national sewing magazines.*

How to Channel-stitch & Shape a Cuff

1) Cut interfacing for cuffs, extending ⅝" (1.5 cm) over center fold. Baste or fuse to wrong side of fabric, on the side that will face outward on garment.

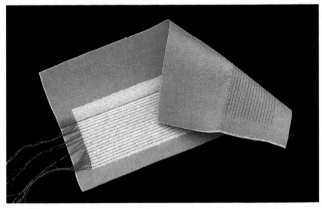

2) Stitch along fold line on right side of fabric using 15 to 20 stitches per inch (2.5 cm); begin and end at seamlines. Stitch parallel lines ⅛" (3 mm) apart; do not stitch in seam allowances. Tie off threads on wrong side.

3) Stitch cuff to sleeve, right sides together. Press seam toward cuff. Grade seam allowances. Fold cuff under at fold line, working from right side of cuff. Turn seam allowances under on long edge and ends, so cuff curves as it will when it is worn. Baste, using silk thread.

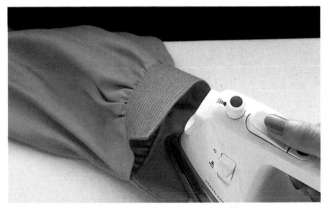

4) Steam inside cuff gently on ironing board, so it shrinks slightly.

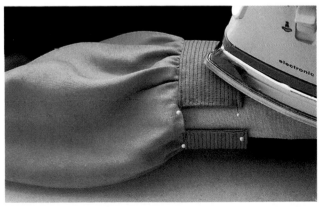

5) Wrap cuff around seam roll. Pin, and gently steam and press from right side. Repeat as necessary to shape cuff. Allow to dry completely.

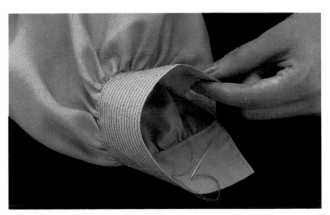

6) Slipstitch long edge and ends of cuff by hand. Cuff will retain shape without excess fabric on inside.

Knit, Cut & Sew

by Susan Guagliumi

With a knitting machine and a sewing machine or serger, you can now make finished sweaters quickly and easily using a method called "knit, cut, and sew." You need not be either an experienced knitter or an expert sewer. The "knit, cut, and sew" method treats machine-knit fabric like purchased yardage. You knit a straight length of fabric, then cut and sew the shaping details into the garment.

"Knit, cut, and sew" is simpler than shaping while machine knitting. You do not need to bother dividing neckline stitches to knit shoulders separately, or worry about matching patterns or color sequences from one garment piece to the next. New knitters find that "knit, cut, and sew" not only saves time, it enables them to knit more elaborate patterns and garments than their beginning skills would normally allow. Experienced knitters agree that it is a great way to alter garments, correct mistakes, and simplify double-bed sweater construction when working with lots of texture or involved patterning. You can also use "knit, cut, and sew" techniques to recycle old garments and create one-of-a-kind combinations with knits and woven fabrics.

A stretch stitch sewn on a conventional sewing machine works fine, but most sewers find that knits are easiest to sew with a serger. Because a serger stitches, trims, and overlocks seams in one operation, the risk of the fabric raveling is minimal. A 4/3-thread serger that has a mock safety stitch is best suited for sewing sweater knits. This gives a secure seam with plenty of stretch. If you use a 3-thread serger, you may want to add a row of stretch stitches using your conventional sewing machine. Although it means an additional step, it is worth doing because it secures the knitted stitches better.

Begin by choosing an appropriate pattern. Sewing patterns that are sized "for knits only" are good choices because they usually avoid fussy details. They have less ease than patterns sized for woven fabrics because the knits provide so much ease of their own. And they generally indicate that seams should be closely trimmed. You can also use knitting patterns, or work from diagrams and garment measurements.

There are two ways to approach "knit, cut, and sew": using straight yardage, or using a "blank." A blank is a rectangle of fabric, knit to the basic size requirements of the pattern, including ribbing or a mock-rib hem. Only the armhole, neckline, and shoulder details need to be cut and sewn.

Whether you knit straight yardage or a blank, remember that although you can use bulky knits for "knit, cut, and sew," finer knits are easier and neater to assemble. Loose knits tend to ravel more easily. Fair Isle floats may not always catch in the seams. Very textured fabrics may cause uneven or skipped stitches. They can all be used — but each situation requires different attention to detail. Perhaps an extra row of safety stitching, an adjustment to the stitch length, or a different presser foot is all it takes. It is always a good idea to knit some extra swatches so you can experiment before committing yourself to making an entire garment.

How Much to Knit

The only way to determine how many stitches to cast on and how many rows to knit is to knit a gauge swatch first. It must be knit in the same yarn, stitch size, and style you plan for the fabric, and should be finished exactly as the garment will be finished. If the garment will be machine washed and dried, then machine wash and dry the swatch; if it will be drycleaned, then steam the swatch.

A garment will knit to the correct size only if the gauge information from which it is knit is accurate. Gauge is measured in stitches or rows per inch (2.5 cm) of fabric. Unfortunately, knitting only one inch (2.5 cm) of fabric will not give an accurate gauge. You need to knit and measure as large a swatch as possible. Most machine knitters work with a gauge swatch that is 40 stitches wide and 60 rows long.

After washing and blocking the swatch, measure 40 stitches, then divide 40 by that measurement to find the stitch gauge. For example, if 40 stitches measure 5½" (14 cm), divide 40 by 5½" (14 cm) to get your stitch gauge of 7.27 stitches per inch (2.86 per cm).

To figure the row gauge, measure from the top to the bottom of the test swatch. Divide 60 rows by that measurement. Do not stretch the swatch as you measure, or round off the numbers; use a calculator if it is complicated. Rounding off measurements can cost you a little here and a little there, making the blank or yardage the wrong size even before you begin. Accurate gauge is the key to successful knitting. There is no reason to knit more fabric than you need, and nothing is more frustrating than coming up short!

To determine how many needles to cast on, multiply your stitch gauge by the width of the largest pattern piece. Determine how many rows to knit by multiplying the row gauge by the combined length of all the pattern pieces. You can knit a few extra rows for insurance, but you should not need many if your swatching and measuring are done carefully.

Or, rather than knit one continuous piece, cast on and knit several different pieces of fabric. This may be a more economical way to accommodate pattern pieces of different widths.

Blanks, like shaped sweaters, must be cast on and knit to the exact width of the garment pieces. Bind off or zigzag the last row of your knitted fabric so it will not ravel when you wash and dry or steam it before cutting.

Cutting Knit Yardage

Although a pattern may contain pieces that say "cut on fold," sweater knits should always be cut on a single thickness of fabric. Trace the pattern to duplicate the missing half so it can be cut out flat.

Make sure you do not stretch the fabric and that you observe the straight grain as you lay out the pattern pieces. Pin pieces with long quilter's pins or T-pins. Use chalk or tailor's tacks rather than cutting notches to mark the fabric.

Initially, it may be scary to cut into a knit, but you will get used to it! In the beginning, you might be more comfortable cutting and finishing the edges on one piece at a time, rather than stacking up a pile of cut

pieces. If using a serger, take advantage of the serger's ability to cut and bind the raw edges of the knit to avoid any possibility of the fabric raveling when you handle it. Try basting a duplicate pattern right to the fabric, then use the serger to cut it out and overlock the edges all at once. If you are working with blanks, you can draw neck, armhole, and shoulder details onto the fabric with tailor's chalk, then serge over the chalk lines. If you don't have a serger, zigzag the raw edges on your conventional sewing machine.

Sewing a Knit Garment

Be careful not to stretch the fabric as you feed it under the presser foot. Fluted "lettuce" edges are more likely to occur when sewing knits on a conventional sewing machine, but you can get them with a serger, too. The trick is to push the fabric under the foot, never holding it taut as you would a woven fabric. Seams stitched on the crosswise grain — along necklines and armholes, for example — are more likely to stretch than those sewn on the lengthwise grain. Stitch these areas slowly and pay close attention to how you feed the fabric.

If you are sewing on a conventional sewing machine, use an Even Feed™ foot. Stitch the seams first with a small zigzag stitch. Then add a row of straight stitches just inside the seam allowance.

When using a serger, you can use the same thread in the loopers that you choose for the needles. You may want to use woolly nylon; it has more stretch than all-purpose thread. If you knit your garment with an evenly twisted lightweight yarn, you may be able to thread it through the upper looper of your serger. Use it to add a decorative edge finish to the garment.

Sew seams according to the allowances and trimming instructions on your pattern. Most knitting patterns allow for very narrow seams. You may want to move the serger blade out of the way when stitching blanks; there is no need to trim with the serger if the piece was knitted to size.

Construction Tips

One of the reasons knitted garments are such a pleasure to wear is that they are fluid and soft. They seldom need to be interfaced or lined. If you feel that a button band or a collar, for example, would hold its shape better with some interfacing, use one of the sew-in varieties and tack it lightly in place. Avoid iron-on interfacings because the heat and weight of the iron tend to flatten knit stitches and may melt or excessively relax some synthetic yarns.

Sewing a knit fabric presents some challenges. Applying pockets, topstitching, and making buttonholes are all easier to do if you use a tear-away stabilizer like tissue or waxed paper under the fabric as you sew.

When you are working with knits that tend to slip and stretch, basting is far more accurate than using pins — and pins can spell disaster for a serger's blade.

Shoulder seams are the primary weight-bearing seams in most garments, and therefore they are the ones most prone to stretch. They often need to be stabilized to retain the garment's shape. You can use ¼" (6 mm) twill tape or ¾" (2 cm) tricot bias binding as a stabilizer, stitching it into the overlocked edge. As you push the knit fabric under the presser foot, hold the stabilizer and stitch through it as you serge or zig-zag. Many machines have a guide that feeds the stabilizer evenly.

Twill tape has no stretch; it is especially suitable for stabilizing seams in coats and heavy, oversized sweaters. Tricot bias binding is a little stretchier; it works well for supporting raglan seams and other bias stitching.

Strips of fusible knit interfacing are wonderful for edges that will be turned and topstitched, and also for securing the cut edges of pieces to be sewn on a sewing machine. Do a test swatch first to make sure that the fusing heat does not melt the fabric.

Finishing the Edges

Facings on knit garments are usually replaced by ribbed, hemmed, or crocheted edges. If you choose to face an edge, you can use knit self-facings or facings cut from woven fabric. Grosgrain ribbon is effective for binding or facing some edges. A crocheted edge is a decorative possibility that can add pizzazz to a neckline or sleeve edge. Ribbing, though, is the most common edge finish for sweaters.

If you are working with purchased ribbings, buy about two-thirds the measurement of the edge to which they will be stitched. If you are knitting ribbed bands yourself, calculate the amount to knit by multiplying the edge measurement by your stockinette stitch gauge. The stockinette gauge is the most reliable figure to use, because the ribbing will naturally draw up to size.

Whenever possible, sew ribbing seams by hand using a blindstitch, also called a Kitchener stitch. It is a small detail, but one that makes a great difference in the look of the completed garment. Particularly at neck and wrists, ribbing joints show up clearly when you are wearing a garment. Hand-sewn ribbing is easy to learn and does not take long to do. Whether ribbing is attached by hand or with a serger or conventional sewing machine, sew the seams in the garment and the ribbing first, then join the ribbing to the garment.

Commercially, "knit, cut, and sew" necklines are finished with a "sandwich band" that encloses the serged edge of the fabric between two neckband layers. Sandwich bands can be backstitched on by hand, some can be attached right on the knitting machine, but the ideal method is with a linking machine.

The linking machine gives home knitters the ability to finish garment edges professionally.

The Linking Machine

Linking machines, or linkers, have always been used in the garment industry. Recently, these machines have become available to home knitters, who are finding that linkers speed up the finishing process and add a professional look to garments.

Most linkers have a rotating drum with about 220 point needles to hold the stitches. The drum rotates past a hook-needle assembly where the linking actually takes place. The machine makes a crochet chain stitch to attach garment sections. Although the size of the stitch is fixed, it can be adjusted somewhat by the amount of tension applied to the yarn as it passes through the tension discs. Linkers are used for seaming as well as applying details like appliqués, pockets, and fancy trimmings. They can gather with elastic, pleat, pin-tuck, and even install zippers. They excel at applying sandwich bands to conceal garment edges. These bands can be knit in plain stockinette, mock rib, or rib. You can even add picot details or buttonholes. Linking machines can add the finishing touch to "knit, cut, and sew" garments.

Susan Guagliumi is a knitting consultant for The Singer Company and contributing editor of Threads *magazine, in which she has published articles on machine knitting.*

Dressed-Up Stretch Knits

by Gail Brown

Imagine sewing that requires no darts, interfacings, facings, pressing, or hand stitching. A simple straight-stitch technique that produces the latest look in fashion silhouettes. Garments that shape and drape beautifully, without wrinkling.

How, you ask? With twin needles and spandex blends, the practical knits that are indispensable to swimmers, joggers, and aerobics enthusiasts.

These days, stretch knits are doing double duty as fabrics for swishy dresses and separates. For busy sewers, stretch knits' newfound versatility is a welcome breakthrough. It makes possible an innovative, streamlined type of sewing: twin-needle seaming and finishing. The fabric makes this process incredibly fast, too, thanks to its 100% stretch and recovery and ravel-free cut edges. After only an hour or two of sewing, you can be wearing a fabulous fashion that fits and moves like no other.

For this fast stretch-seaming method, all you need are twin needles and a zigzag sewing machine that threads from the front to the back. If you are uncertain about a machine's adaptability to twin-needle stitching, ask your dealer. The main advantage of twin-needle stitching is stretchability. The bobbin thread zigzags on the underside of the fabric, resulting in a straight stitch that is stretchy. Even when subjected to rigorous stretching, these stitches seldom break. Twin-needle straight stitching rivals 3-thread serging in durability and stretchability.

Borrow inspiration for styles to sew from trendy ready-to-wear catalogs and boutiques. Look for "spandex" (the generic fiber name) or "Lycra®" (DuPont's trademarked name for spandex) on the fiber-content label or in the description. Garment ideas are as diverse as they are enticing. For the young at heart, body-conscious cropped tops, leggings, and minis are the rage. But the stretch-fashion spectrum also includes sophisticated, full-skirted dresses for office or evening, many of which carry the trendy Betsey Johnson label. Designer Donna Karan likes Lycra/wool blends for her elegant surplice wrap tops. Seventh Avenue's latest novelty is leather or fur and stretch knit combinations; panels of Lycra-blend knit are interspersed throughout a garment for contouring and comfort.

There are many pattern choices for Lycra-blend stretch knits. Obviously, the shape is a clue to suitability: smooth-fitting garments without apparent darts, princess seaming, or elastics are good candidates for stretch knits. Your next clues to stretch-knit suitability are the stretch gauge and fabric suggestions printed on the back of the pattern envelope. Patterns designed expressly for this fabric category will specify 50% or more stretch in the crosswise and possibly the lengthwise directions — a 4" (10 cm) section must stretch at least 2" (5 cm) — and will list two-way stretch knits under fabric recommendations.

Patterns designed "for knits only" — styles requiring 25% stretch — also work well. The extra stretchability of Lycra blends offers performance bonuses like better wrinkle resistance and drapability, plus faster sewing (facings generally can be eliminated). One caution, though: avoid styles with severe curves, like deeply scooped necklines. It is difficult to finish such edges smoothly using the twin-needle technique.

The garment description on the back of the pattern envelope is your best guide to intended fit and length. Adjectives like "close-fitting" or "tight-fitting," typical on junior sportswear patterns, mean that little or no ease has been allowed. Superstretchy Lycra-blend single knits cannot be beat for comfort in body-fitting fashions. "Semi-fitted" or "loose-fitting" garments have more ease allowed and generally are more flattering to postadolescent figures.

Tips for Sewing Lycra®-blend Knits

Prewash or dryclean the fabric according to the care instructions. For washable fabrics, machine wash at a warm temperature and tumble dry at a low setting. Bleach and extra-hot washer or dryer temperatures are potentially destructive to spandex.

Eliminate center front and back seams by cutting pieces on a fold. Create two new fold lines — one at each side — by bringing the selvage edges together in the middle of the fabric.

Refold the fabric when laying out the pattern to avoid permanent fold lines. If they cannot be avoided, position them where they will not be seen or where they look natural, like down the center of the sleeves.

Follow "with nap" pattern layouts, if possible. Most knits have a discernible one-way knit construction that causes shading.

Cut fabric with sharp shears rather than a rotary cutter. A rotary blade can pull the fabric, distorting the shape and the seam accuracy.

Plan your layout on a surface large enough for the full length and width of the fabric. If allowed to hang over the edge of a table, the knit will stretch, causing inaccurate cutting.

Secure the pattern pieces with weights or long, large-headed pins.

Tips for Sewing with Twin Needles

Buy at least three twin needles — the two extra are backups in case of blunting or breakage. Use size 80/12 needles set 4 mm apart, if possible. Size 90/14, set either 4 mm or 3 mm apart, are also suitable. Twin needles set less than 3 mm apart are not suitable for sewing stretch knits.

Change the twin needle immediately if the point becomes blunted. A blunt-ended needle can make permanent holes in your fabric. Skipped stitches may also signal the need for a new needle.

Use all-purpose polyester or cotton-wrapped polyester thread. Place the two spools on the top of your sewing machine so they unwind in alternate directions to minimize tangling.

Check the clearance of the twin needle through your presser foot and needle plate by turning the flywheel slowly by hand before you start to sew.

Adjust the tension of the top threads by sewing on a scrap of fabric before you begin. Usually, the needle tension will need to be tightened.

Remember that Lycra-blend stretch knits not only stretch 100%, but recover completely. Even if you have been using a smaller pattern size for sewing the very stretchy but less-resilient cotton interlocks, do not apply the same sizing-down strategy to stretch knits. For fitting and sewing insurance, allow 1" (2.5 cm) seams and trim off the excess later. The larger seam allowance will make stitching seams more accurate, too.

In response to the ready-to-wear stretch knit craze, many fabric retailers and mail-order sources now are carrying the once hard-to-find Lycra blends. Solid colors make up the majority of current selections, but stripes and prints are not uncommon finds, especially from stores and suppliers specializing in knits. Comfortable cotton or cotton-polyester/Lycra blends are your best bets for daytime clothes; shiny nylon/Lycras are dramatic for dress-up or dancing. Other blends may be more available soon, including luxurious combinations of Lycra and wool, rayon, or silk.

With few exceptions, stretch knits are 58/60" (147.5/152.5 cm) wide, but the weight, fiber percentages, and stretchability can vary considerably. Most are single knits that owe their stretch to the Lycra, which can be about 8% to 20% of the blend. The more Lycra, the more stretch and recovery.

Before you buy, test the stretch of any Lycra-blend knit, not only for pattern compatibility but also to judge its performance under wearing conditions. Does it spring back or remain stretched out? Does it stretch at least 25%, according to the stretch gauge on the pattern? (Don't worry if it stretches more, as long as the fabric recovers well.) Keep in mind that the twin-needle sewing methods outlined here rely on at least 25% stretch. If the knit does not stretch to the pattern gauge, the finished garment can be too tight, distorted, or impossible to pull on over your head or hips. Also, before the salesclerk cuts your yardage, open the fabric out flat to look for permanent fold lines, recurring flaws, or needle holes.

Gail Brown is the Contributing Editor for The Serger Update *and* The Sewing Update *newsletters. She has written six sewing books, her most recent being* Gail Brown's Book of Sewing and Serging Knits.

How to Stitch a Twin-needle Seam

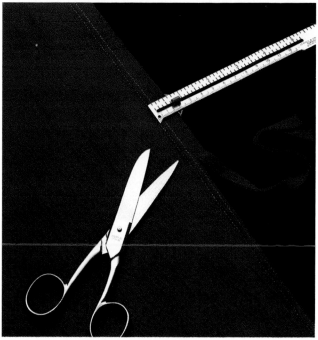

1) Insert twin needle in machine. Use general-purpose presser foot and needle plate. Test for safe clearance of needle through presser foot and needle plate by turning the flywheel slowly by hand. Thread machine according to instruction manual. Adjust tension.

2) Stitch seams. Do not stretch as you sew; the seam is naturally stretchy. After seaming and checking fit, trim close to the stitching line nearest the fabric edge. Press seam to one side.

How to Sew a Twin-needle Edge Finish

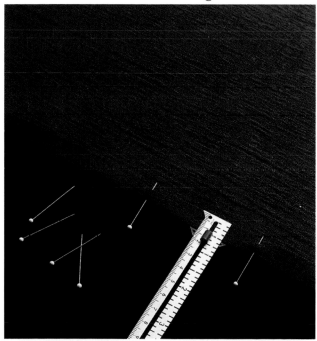

1) Turn the raw edge under ½" to ⅝" (1.3 to 1.5 cm). Lightly press. Pin perpendicular to fold, as necessary.

2) Topstitch from the right side, using twin needle, ⅜" (1 cm) from the folded edge. Trim the excess allowance close to stitching, if necessary.

Home Fashions

Home Fashions Outlook

by Laura W. Rehrmann

Singer/songwriter Peter Allen's popular refrain, "cuz everything old is new again," could be the theme song of home decorating this year. Comfortable Americana styles, English chintz hominess, and a general rounding off of harsh, angular, contemporary edges mark the best of home decorating styles today. One word describes this look: eclectic. The most exciting rooms blend styles rather than slavishly following one theme.

"The customer today has a more refined taste level and higher expectations," says Jan Jessup, director of purchasing for the 68-store Calico Corner® retail chain. The media have had a profound impact on our idea of what looks good. Television, movies, and magazines have made other cultures familiar to us. Now we want to pick and choose among a vast array of ethnic as well as historical colors, furniture, and fabrics to decorate our homes.

Today's Styles

There are three main styles popular in interior design today: English, Contempory, and American Country. Of the three, the English style — full of chintz, flowered prints, and layers of fabric — is the most important home decorating influence.

"The English look is really eclectic, and that's why people embrace it," says designer Judy Davison. "English style evolved as England colonized the world. Prints depicting the flowers and birds of the New World, bamboo furniture and blue-and-white porcelain from China, and paisley and rattan from India were put into a melting pot which produced the delightful mixture that marks the English style."

More than any other, the English style has to do with fabric. Windows are fully dressed with curtains, fabric-covered rods, pleats, ruffles, and bias trims. Pillows are detailed with ruffles and welting. Beds are topped with canopies and skirted with one or two layers of dust ruffles. Chairs and sofas have longer, more graceful skirts, making the standard 5" (12.5 cm) skirt look chopped off and short.

Another style in decorating today is Contemporary. But the angular, hard-edged design of earlier Contemporary furniture is rounded, curved, and overstuffed. The rounded forms of the 1930s — like the opulent swells of an old Buick or comfortable club chairs — are updated in smooth, cotton fabrics. Stripes, small geometric prints, and lightly textured linen fabrics are good contemporary decorating choices. The finishing details are often classic: ruffles are replaced by tailored box pleats on bed skirts, table coverings, and pillows. Postmodern influences creep in, too, as in fabric draped at the window and caught at the side, or in loose, slouchy slipcovers.

American Country is the final decorating style for this year. Three distinct themes run through American Country decorating: English, contemporary, and quaint.

The English variation on American Country abounds with flowery chintzes, sweet-pea colors, cheery ceramics, and wicker furniture.

Contemporary-themed American Country decorating is light and modern, with weathered pine furniture, painted floors, and crisp patterns of white-on-dark backgrounds or the reverse. This theme is strongly influenced by American folk art: weathervanes, painted wood watermelon wedges, and large baskets are some of the accents you will find in these rooms.

The quaint look of the third American Country theme is achieved using collectibles, antiques, dark woods, and calico prints. Cozy, dark rooms are filled with collections reflecting the owner's interests. Polished dark wood furniture gleams, complemented by ruffles and laces on pillows, tablecloths, and curtains.

Fabrics

In many ways, home decorating today is all about fabric. And the selection of fabrics has never been better. Customers have demanded better quality and more refined designs. Mills have responded by updating antiquated machinery. In the last five years, jacquard mills have done twenty years' worth of modernizing. The increased capabilities of new looms and computerized designing make it easy for mills to produce an incredible variety of fabric styles in an enormous range of colors.

Fabrics to watch for include English chintz, still a strong favorite. Working from old documents, scraps of embroidered linen, patterns on china and ceramics, and botanical prints, mills continue to produce new English garden looks ranging from detailed floral prints to soft, blowsy roses.

New this season are paisleys richly detailed with subtle metallic touches which make the fabrics exciting but never glitzy.

Contemporary Style

Photograph courtesy of Waverly Fabrics

English variation on American Country Style

Tapestries are very strong on furniture. Tapestry-print themes include urns, stylized flowers, birds, animals, and woodland themes.

Along with the look of softer interiors and lots of fabric, lace has made a steady comeback. Lace tablecloths hanging to the floor over circular tables; lace curtains, either café or sweeping to floor-length; lace pillows and bed skirts — however it is used, lace fabric gives a room texture and softness in one step. Lace fits any decorating scheme, from the most modern to the most traditional.

Stripes are used in American Country, English, and Contemporary styles. Polka dots figure strongly in Contemporary styles. Trompe l'oeil effects (which give the illusion of three dimensions), marbled fabrics, animal-skin prints, and upholstery-weight Ultra-suede® are important fabrics in pulling together a Contemporary-style room.

Colors

Strong, rich pastels continue to be the best-selling colors in all collections, according to Jessup. Peach, coral, mauve, rose, and the newest pastel, yellow, are all important pastel themes. Greens with blue tones and blues with green tones continue to be popular colors. What you won't find are the yellow-toned "hot" greens that are neon bright. Red, especially lacquer red, is an exciting new color this year.

Don't be timid when choosing color schemes for a room. Color charges a room with excitement and vitality. Color is the foundation of successful interiors. The rooms we like best reflect the confident and stylish use of color, a talent learned by experimentation.

There are three basic types of color schemes: one-color, related-color, and complementary-color schemes. The easiest to choose is a one-color scheme combining different tones of the same color. Think of a room decorated in natural, ivory, and ecru tones.

Linen, lace, and muslin could carry the color theme through curtains, pillows, and upholstery. Choose a single accent color like terra cotta, black, or aquamarine for pillows. An upholstered chair or sofa might incorporate all the tones in a single print to unify the room.

A second color option is to use related colors. Many fabric prints include a wonderful combination of colors. Pick prints you like and combine them with solids to chart a color scheme. Pick out a particular color from the prints and repeat it somewhere else in the room.

The third option is the boldest and often the most interesting to the eye. This color scheme uses complementary colors, those opposite each other on the color wheel. Purple and yellow, blue and orange, and red and green create exciting contrasts. White, black, and gray accents enhance complementary colors.

Details

Dressmaking details in interior fashions are another hallmark of expertly styled rooms. Details like welting, ruffles, ribbon ties, trims, fringes, shaped valances, swags, jabots, tiebacks, and luxurious draping give windows a custom look today.

Interlining draperies and curtains with flannel is the key to luxurious weight, body, and drape in a window treatment. "Interlining gives chintz, silk, satin, or any other lightweight fabric a million-dollar look," says Jessup.

Swagging windows with a long length of fabric tucked and looped around a rod is a look that fits with any decorating style. The same treatment may be used to create elegant bed canopies. Jessup suggests sewing two fabrics back-to-back. Line a bold print or solid fabric with a jacquard or small-print lining in a contrasting color. Then use tiebacks or swagging to fold back the draperies and reveal the lining.

Balloon shades also create a luxurious finish to a window. Like any curtain, they should be lined; an insulated lining gives them great body.

In upholstery, watch for pleated or ruffled skirts on chairs and sofas; darts in cushions and corners to sculpt fabric; and single or double welting to outline the edges. The creative use of stripes — combining vertical, horizontal, and bias stripes in a single chair, for example — is another dressmaking detail making the transition to the home decorating arena.

Where to Start

When you are getting ready to redo a room or start from scratch, where do you begin? Davison advises you to think of interior design as similar to planning, and then building, a wardrobe.

Begin by educating yourself. Tear out magazine photos of furniture, window coverings, colors — any details

you like. Find a bookstore with a good home decorating section and browse through the titles. Buy the book that describes the look that appeals to you most. Study the photographs in order to understand what colors, furniture styles, and details make the style complete. Many books include construction details and sources for the fabrics shown, so you could choose an interior you like and copy it exactly.

Once you settle on a theme, proceed as you would to build a wardrobe. Buy one fabulous piece — furniture, pottery, a quilt, or perhaps a small Oriental rug to put in front of the sofa. Use colors from that one central piece for pillows, drapes, and paint. A beautiful vase of flowers, a collection of china plates, or a good painting might be another source for colors to repeat in the room.

"Think simply. Be selective," Davison says. "If you have a small budget, splurge on one good piece. It might be silk flowers rather than cheap plastic ones. Four pillows made from $50-a-yard fabric can make an ordinary sofa look like a million."

As you build your interior, continue to ask yourself why you like a certain style, color, or pattern. Define the look you want more precisely. Ask salespeople in fabric stores for advice. And if you hesitate to make final choices yourself, call on a professional interior designer to help you get the room you want. You can consult with someone for just a few hours, or turn over the whole project to a professional. (Call wholesale showrooms for some names.) In the end, you will have an interior that reflects your taste and style and is professionally pulled together.

No Better Time Than Now

Turning bare rooms into the stylish rooms you want can be an awesome project. Whether you are looking for a sleek and sophisticated or a casual and comfortable effect, you want to make your home welcoming and warm. The possibilities for sewing home fashions yourself have never been better. Books, magazines, professional help, and the wealth of new fabrics widely available today make it possible for you to design and execute the room you have pictured.

For Further Reading:
Sewing for the Home and *More Sewing for the Home*, Singer Sewing Reference Library®. *Fabric Magic*, Paine. *Decorating with Fabric Liberty Style*, Watkins. *Laura Ashley Windows*, Wilhide.

Laura Rehrmann is a freelance writer specializing in sewing and fashion topics.

Clustered Gathers: A New Bed Skirt & Sham Design

by Kathleen Ellingson

A new and attractive bed skirt consists of a skirt interrupted by soft clusters of gathers at each corner of the bed and along the sides and foot. It is a good style for master bedrooms since it combines the tailored look of a box-pleated skirt with the softness of a gathered skirt. Make one in a rich cotton chintz for a dramatic look, or in a wide eyelet with an embroidered, scalloped hem for a light and airy touch. Or, use flat sheets that coordinate with the rest of your bedding for a total look that is often inexpensive to sew.

To continue the look of tailored softness, make a matching sham with gathers clustered at the corners. Border the sham in a single or a double flange; select fabrics to highlight colors and patterns in the rest of your bedding. A row of solid-colored piping adds a professional-looking finishing touch. If you use sheets for the bed skirt, you might make the pillow flange from the contrasting border or ruffles that often finish the top of a flat sheet. Or use lace or eyelet trim with a prefinished edge for the narrow upper flange, and fabric for the lower flange.

Consider fabric weight as you plan your bed skirt and sham design. The heavier the fabric, the less dense the gathers. Lightweight fabric is easiest to work with. For the flanged sham particularly, consider fabric weight. The flange fabric should have enough body to stand out from the sham, but the more layers and weight, the harder it will be to gather the fabric tightly in the corners. One way to eliminate some bulk on a sham is to use a single layer of fabric for one or both of the flanges, finishing the edges with a narrow or rolled hem.

Kathleen Ellingson owns and operates Davis Design, a design studio and workroom in Chicago, Illinois, providing custom-sewn home furnishings to interior designers, store accounts, and individual clients.

Supplies

Decorator fabric or sheets.

Flat sheet for bed skirt deck (twin-size for twin, full, or queen bed; full-size for king bed).

Zipper for sham, about 3" (7.5 cm) shorter than length of sham.

5/32" cording for welting on sham.

✂ Cutting Directions

Measure drop (from top of box spring to floor), width, and length of box spring.

Cut depth of bed skirt is drop plus 2¼" (5.6 cm); this allows for ¼" (6 mm) clearance at the floor.

Cut length of bed skirt is two times length plus width plus 25" (63.5 cm) for each cluster of gathers: one in each corner, two on each side, and one (two for king-size bed) at the foot. Twin, full, and queen-size beds will need nine clusters of gathers; king-size, ten clusters. Seams should be calculated to fall at the beginning or the end of a gathered section.

Cut deck is 1" (2.5 cm) wider and 1" (2.5 cm) longer than box spring.

How to Sew a Bed Skirt with Clustered Gathers

1) Cut deck. Fold in half lengthwise, then crosswise, so all four corners are together. Cut through all four layers to curve corners, using a saucer as a guide.

2) Fold curved corners in half to determine centers. Cut notch through all layers at center line.

3) Fold the deck in half lengthwise and then into thirds. Notch deck sides at folds on cut edges through layers to mark placement for clustered gathers.

4) Fold deck lengthwise, in half for twin, full, or queen; in thirds for king. Notch deck foot at folds on cut edges through layers to mark placement for clustered gathers.

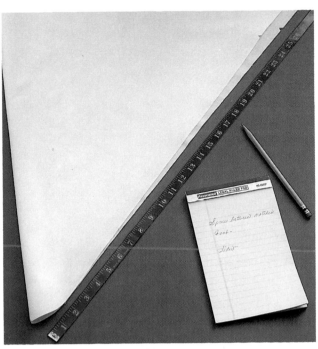

5) Measure and record distance between notches in deck. The spaces between notches at the foot may not be exactly the same as spaces between notches at the sides.

6) Cut skirt pieces. Remember to position seams at beginning or end of gathering spaces. Mark adjacent seams in seam allowances.

7) Stitch skirt sections together to form one length, using ½" (1.3 cm) seam allowances; finish edges. Stitch double-fold 1" (2.5 cm) hem on lower edge; stitch double-fold ¼" (6 mm) hems on side edges.

(Continued on next page)

How to Sew a Bed Skirt with Clustered Gathers (continued)

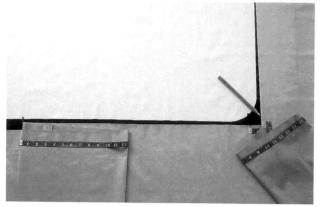

8) Mark placement of gathers on skirt according to measurements, step 5; begin at center of foot section. Hide any variation in measurement within gathers. Mark vertical stitching lines from upper edge to middle of bed skirt at each gathering placement mark.

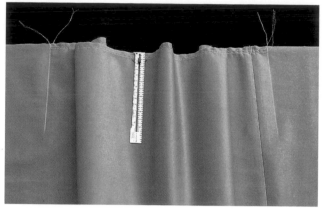

9) Stitch two rows of bastestitching or zigzag over a cord between vertical marks in spaces to be gathered. Stitch within the ½" (1.3 cm) seam allowance.

10) Pin each gathered section along marked vertical lines, wrong sides together. Stitch along markings from upper edge to center, except at the four corners. At corners, stitch from upper edge for ¾" (2 cm) only.

11) Pull gathering threads to gather tightly. Center, flatten, and pin each cluster of gathers to skirt edge. Baste across gathers to secure.

12) Pin skirt to deck, matching notches to center of gathers; stitch. Serge or zigzag edges around entire deck. Press seam allowances toward deck.

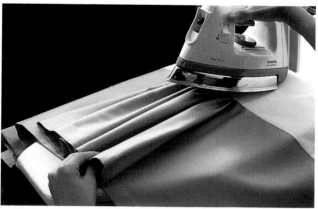

13) Steam each gathered cluster, to create soft vertical folds.

✂ Cutting Directions

For sham front, cut fabric 1" (2.5 cm) wider and 1" (2.5 cm) longer than pillow.

For sham back, cut fabric 1" (2.5 cm) wider and 3" (7.5 cm) longer than pillow.

For each flange, cut two strips of fabric: cut length of each strip is equal to length plus width of cut sham front plus 15" (38 cm), and cut width is equal to two times finished width of flange plus 1" (2.5 cm).

Suggested finished width of lower flange is 4½" (11.5 cm), and suggested finished width of upper flange, 3½" (9 cm); lower flange should be 1" (2.5 cm) wider than upper flange.

For each sham, cut welting strip 1½" (3.8 cm) wide, by two times the length plus two times the width of pillow, plus extra for joining. Cut ⁵⁄₃₂" cording the same length as welting strip.

How to Sew a Double-flange Pillow Sham

1) Cut a 3½" (9 cm) zipper strip from one long edge on sham back. Serge or zigzag one long edge of strip and sham back. Press under 1" (2.5 cm) on finished edge of back and ½" (1.3 cm) on finished edge of strip.

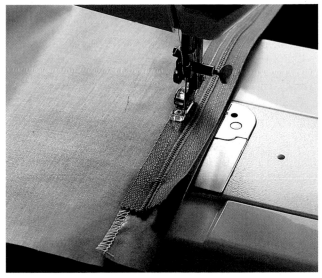

2) Place closed zipper face down on 1" (2.5 cm) seam allowance, with edge of zipper tape on fold. Using zipper foot, stitch inside edge next to zipper teeth, backstitching at each end.

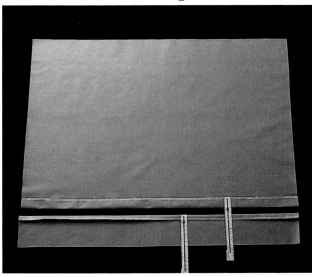

3) Turn right side up. Place pressed edge of zipper strip along edge of teeth on other side of zipper. Stitch close to edge.

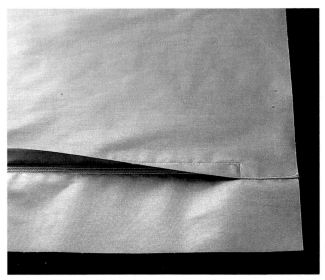

4) Stitch across each end of zipper; pivot, and continue stitching through all layers to side edges.

(Continued on next page)

How to Sew a Double-flange Pillow Sham (continued)

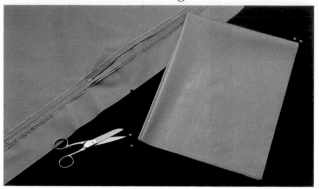

5) Fold sham front and back in half; fold again to quarter. Mark fold lines at center of each side edge with a notch. Open zipper partway.

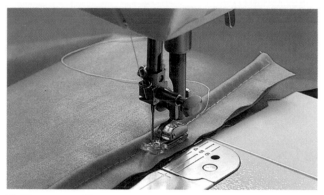

6) Center cording on wrong side of welting strip; fold strip over cording, aligning raw edges; stitch close to cording, using zipper foot. Place welting on right side of sham front, with end of cording ½" (1.3 cm) from center of lower edge and with raw edges even. Stitch scant ½" (1.3 cm) seam, beginning 2" (5 cm) from end of strip.

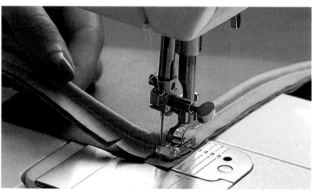

7) Clip seam allowance of welting strip as you approach each corner. Turn corner, with needle down through all layers. At each corner, hold layers at previous corner and pull gently so cording slips back into position.

8) Stop stitching 4" (10 cm) from starting point. Trim cording and welting strip, allowing ½" (1.3 cm) for seam allowance. Remove stitching from welting ends. Stitch ends together. Finger press seam open. Butt cording; finish stitching welting to sham front.

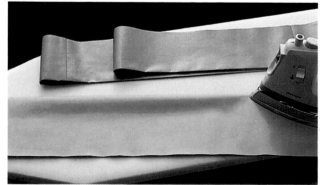

9) Stitch ends of each flange together to form two continuous loops. Press seams open. Fold in half lengthwise, with wrong sides together and raw edges even; press.

10) Align one flange with long edge of sham front so seamline of flange is 3½" (9 cm) beyond cut edge of sham front. Cut a notch in flange opposite notch in sham. Repeat for remaining flange.

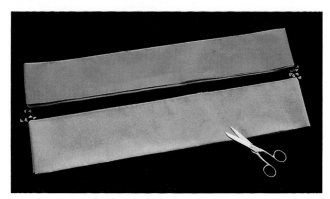

11) Fold flange at notch. Cut a notch at opposite fold-line. Fold flange in half again to quarter; notch fold-lines. Repeat for remaining flange.

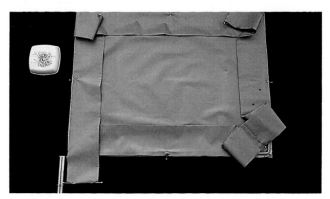

12) Align notches on one flange with notches on sham at center of each side. Seamlines of flange will be at opposite corners. Mark corners of flange with pins. Repeat for remaining flange.

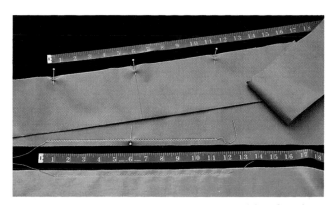

13) Zigzag over heavy thread on wrong side of each flange, beginning and ending 5½" (14 cm) on either side of corner pins. Leave 3" (7.5 cm) thread tails at each end.

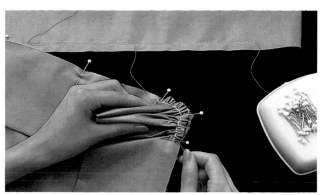

14) Pin narrow flange to front, matching notches. Draw up gathers so flange fits sham front. Wrap threads around pins to secure; machine-baste at corners only. Place wide flange over narrow flange; gather and pin.

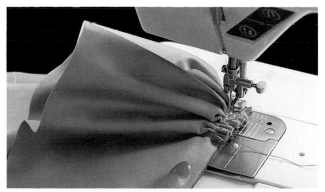

15) Machine-baste through all layers ⅜" (1 cm) from raw edge, using zipper foot. Pound layers with hammer to flatten before stitching, if necessary.

16) Place sham front and back right sides together, with front on top; pin. Stitch around sham ½" (1.3 cm) from edge. Serge or zigzag raw edges. Turn right side out; steam gathers. Insert pillow.

Simple Slipcovers for Folding Chairs

by Mev Jenson and Amy Engman

A smart-looking slipcover is an easy and affordable way to dress up an old steel folding chair.

For special occasions, for a change of seasons, or simply for some fun in home decorating, folding-chair slipcovers are attractive and versatile. They can work with any decorating scheme from contemporary to country, depending upon fabric choice and styling options. And they offer a practical solution to the age-old problem posed by large gatherings: attractive yet portable and stowable temporary seating.

Folding chairs come in a variety of shapes and sizes, quite similar but not exactly the same. To make a well-fitting slipcover you need a pattern for your chair. Make a custom-fitted pattern out of muslin. Start with four rectangles of fabric cut approximately to size, then drape and pin them to the chair to fine-tune the shape. Once this muslin has been fitted, use it as a pattern for cutting the slipcover.

When you make the actual slipcover, add a decorative bow tied across the back, or you may want to add contrasting piping or ruffles — whatever creative touches you like to make the design your own.

Mev Jenson and Amy Engman are co-owners of Textilis, a fabric and decorating business in Minneapolis. Mev has degrees in education and counseling, and enjoys sewing, reading, and writing. Amy has a degree in textiles and 15 years' experience in the textile industry. She is an accomplished seamstress in the home decorating and clothing fields.

Supplies

3 yards (2.75 m) unbleached muslin, 42" (107 cm) wide, for pattern.

Folding chair.

Marker or pencil, pins, shears, double-stick tape.

Heavy weight, such as books or gallon (3.78 l) bottle of water.

Decorator fabric.

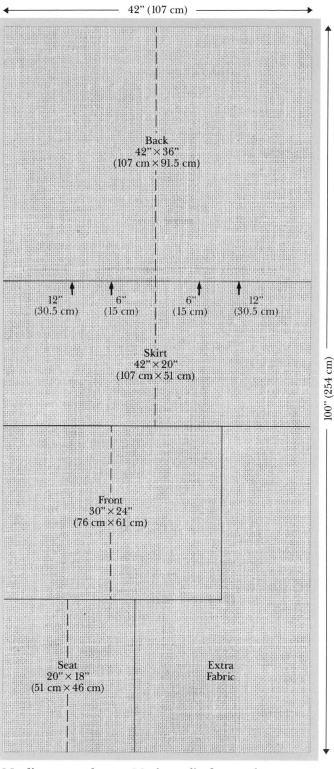

Muslin pattern layout. Mark muslin for rough pattern pieces; cut on solid lines. Mark dotted center lines. Mark arrows on skirt pattern piece, 6" (15 cm) and 12" (30.5 cm) on each side of center line.

How to Make a Folding Chair Slipcover

1) Pin back and front pattern pieces together for 4" (10 cm) on either side of center marks. Pin horizontally from center toward sides, using a ½" (1.3 cm) seam allowance.

2) Drape pinned pattern over chair, matching center lines to center of chair back. Secure pattern at top of chair back with double-stick tape. Tuck pattern under back legs; keep grainline straight.

3) Push front pattern piece toward back edge of seat at bottom to allow enough ease for sitting. Secure pattern to chair with double-stick tape at center of seat and both corners.

4) Drape back pattern around curve of chair. Drape smoothly, keeping grainline perpendicular to floor. Pin along edge of chair to indicate seamline. Repeat for other side.

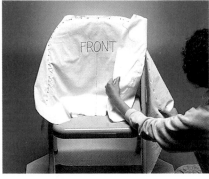

5) Drape front pattern around curve of chair. Pin along edge of chair to indicate seamline. Pin back pattern to front pattern along seamlines, adjusting to fit chair smoothly and maintain grainline.

6) Trace edge of chair seat at bottom of front pattern. Trim to 1" (2.5 cm) beyond traced outline.

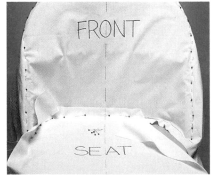

7) Secure seat pattern to chair at center front with double-stick tape. Pin back of seat pattern to bottom of front pattern, stopping where front and back pieces meet.

8) Trace outline of chair seat onto seat pattern. Add ¼" (6 mm) to front edge of seat pattern to allow for rounded front edge of chair. Trim to 1" (2.5 cm) beyond outline.

9) Gather or pleat skirt pattern between 6" and 12" (15 and 30.5 cm) marks on each side of center line. Draw up each set of gathers to 3" (7.5 cm).

10) Weight pattern pieces on chair so they do not move — a gallon (3.78 l) of water or stack of books works well. Match center lines of seat and skirt patterns. Pin skirt to seat, ending where all four pieces meet.

11) Turn up and pin hem to desired length. Pin skirt to back pattern at sides. Examine fit of muslin on chair and make any necessary adjustments. Pattern should fit snugly, without pulling.

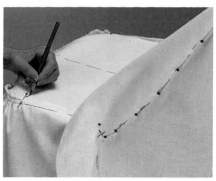

12) Mark seamlines between pins on all pieces. Mark placement for gathers on seat and skirt patterns. Mark all pieces with an "X" at point where all four pattern pieces meet at sides.

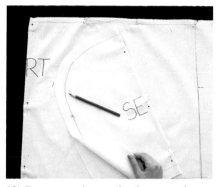

13) Remove pins and release gathers. Lay pieces flat. Mark seamlines. Fold pieces along centers. Compare markings on each half. Make any necessary adjustments so pattern is symmetrical.

14) Trim hem allowance on skirt to 2" (5 cm) for a finished 1" (2.5 cm) double-fold hem.

15) Re-pin, and try pattern on chair. Adjust fit, seamlines, and placement marks, as necessary. Add ½" (1.3 cm) seam allowances; trim excess fabric. Try pattern on chair again, if desired.

16) Cut chair cover from decorator fabric, using muslin pieces as pattern. Transfer markings.

17) Cut two pieces for ties, each 7" (18 cm) wide and 42" (107 cm) long. Fold in half lengthwise, right sides together. Fold one end to form triangle; cut on fold. Stitch cut side and bias end; turn and press.

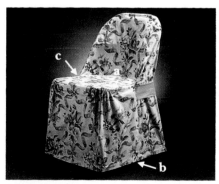

18) Stitch front to seat along back edge of seat between Xs **(a)**. Stitch back to skirt at side seams, inserting tie in seam **(b)**. Gather skirt between markings; stitch front/seat to back/skirt **(c)**. Stitch hem.

Sources

Artists

Patricia Cox, 6601 Normandale Blvd., Minneapolis, MN 55435

Caryl Bryer Fallert, The Bryer Patch Studio, 2031 Collins Rd., Oswego, IL 60543

Jan Faulkner-Wagoner, Jan Faulkner Leather Artist, 816 23rd Ave., Seattle, WA 98122

Tim Harding, 2402 University Ave., St. Paul, MN 55114

LaVonne Horner, 2024 Charlton Ridge, West St. Paul, MN 55118

Marit Lee Kucera, M'ART Designs, 30 St. Albans, #5, St. Paul, MN 55105

Debra Millard Lunn, 1225 Garfield St., Denver, CO 80206

Yvonne Porcella, Porcella Studios, 3619 Shoemake Ave., Modesto, CA 95351

Fabrics, Notions & Supplies

Blue Feather Products, 165 Reiten Dr., Ashland, OR 97520 (magnetic notions)

Clotilde®, Inc., 1909 SW First Ave., Fort Lauderdale, FL 33315 (lightweight nylon thread, One-Step Needle Threader)

Clover Needlecraft, Inc., 1007 E. Dominguez St., Suite N, Carson, CA 90746 (Chaco-liner)

Creative Fibers, 5416 Penn Ave. S., Minneapolis, MN 55419 (marbling chemicals & airbrush medium)

The Crowning Touch, Inc., 2410 Glory C Rd., Medford, OR 97501 (Fasturn® tool)

Distlefink Designs, Inc., P.O. Box 358, Pelham, NY 10803 (magnetic notions)

Dritz Corporation, P.O. Box 5028, Spartanburg, SC 29304 (platinum-plated needles)

G-Street Fabrics, 11854 Rockville Pike, Rockville, MD 20852 (fabrics)

Gingher® Inc., P.O. Box 8865, Greensboro, NC 27419 (Gingher® curved-blade embroidery scissors)

HAPCO Products, 46 Mapleview Dr., Columbia, MO 65203 (platinum-plated needles)

Homebound Company, 23004 Woodinville-Snonomish Highway, Woodinville, WA 98072 (magnetic notions)

June Tailor, Inc., P.O. Box 208, Richfield, WI 53076 (free-arm sleeve board)

Kreinik Manufacturing Company, Inc., P.O. Box 1966, Parkersburg, WV 26102 (platinum-plated needles)

Métier de Gèneve, Elna, Inc., 7642 Washington Ave. S., Minneapolis, MN 55344 (Ribbon Thread™)

Nancy's Notions®, Ltd., 333 Beichl Ave., Beaver Dam, WI 53916 (magnetic notions bar, Sew-Rite® Shape Weights™)

Sew-Art International, 412 S. 425 W., Bountiful, UT 84010 (lightweight nylon thread)

Speed Stitch, 3113-D Broadpoint Dr., Harbor Heights, FL 33983 (Ribbon Thread™)

Stacy Industries Inc., 38 Passaic St., Wood-Ridge, NJ 07075 (Easy-Knit® Straight Cut & Bias Cut)

Tacony Corporation, 1760 Gilsinn Ln., Fenton, MO 63026 (Sew-Rite® Shape Weights™)

Treadleart, 25834 Narbonne Ave., Lomita, CA 90717 (lightweight nylon thread)

United Notions, 13795 Hutton at Landry, Dallas, TX 75234 (magnetic notions)

Velcro USA, Inc., 406 Brown Ave., Manchester, NH 03103 (Velcro® Brand Iron-On Hook & Loop Fastener)

W.H. Collins, Inc., 21 Leslie Ct., Whippany, NJ 07981 (platinum-plated needles)

YLI Corporation, 45 W. 300 N., Provo, UT 84601 (lightweight nylon thread)

Publications

Clothing Care & Repair, More Sewing for the Home, The Perfect Fit, Sewing

Activewear, Sewing for Children, Sewing Essentials, Sewing for the Home, Sewing with a Serger, Sewing Specialty Fabrics, Sewing for Style, Sewing Update No. 1, Tailoring, Timesaving Sewing; Singer Sewing Reference Library®

Catalog Sources — News and Updates, P.O. Box 6232-SS, Augusta, GA 30906

FIBERARTS, 50 College St., Asheville, NC 28801

The Fiberworks Source Book, McRae

Handmade, 50 College St., Asheville, NC 28801

Quilter's Newsletter Magazine, Box 394, Wheatridge, CO 80033

The Serger Update and *The Sewing Update,* Update Newsletters, 2269 Chestnut, Suite 269, San Francisco, CA 94123

The Sew & Save Source Book, Boyd

Sew News, P.O. Box 3134, Harlan, IA 51593-4200

Threads, The Taunton Press, 63 S. Main St., Box 355, Newtown, CT 06470-9989

Treadleart, 25834 Narbonne Ave., Lomita, CA 90717

Groups & Networks

American Craft Council, 401 Park Ave. S., New York, NY 10016

American Sewing Guild, National Headquarters, Box 50936, Indianapolis, IN 46250

Surface Design Association, Inc., 311 E. Washington St., Fayetteville, TN 37334

Cy DeCosse Incorporated offers fine sewing accessories to subscribers. For information write:

Sewing Accessories
5900 Green Oak Drive
Minnetonka, MN 55343